Introvert

An Essential Guide to Making the Most of Your Introversion, including a Guide to Overcoming Social Anxiety and Leadership Tips for Introverts

Contents

Part 1: Introverts

The Ultimate Guide for Introverts Who Don't Want to Change their Quiet Nature but Still Make Friends, Be Sociable, and Develop Powerful Leadership Skills

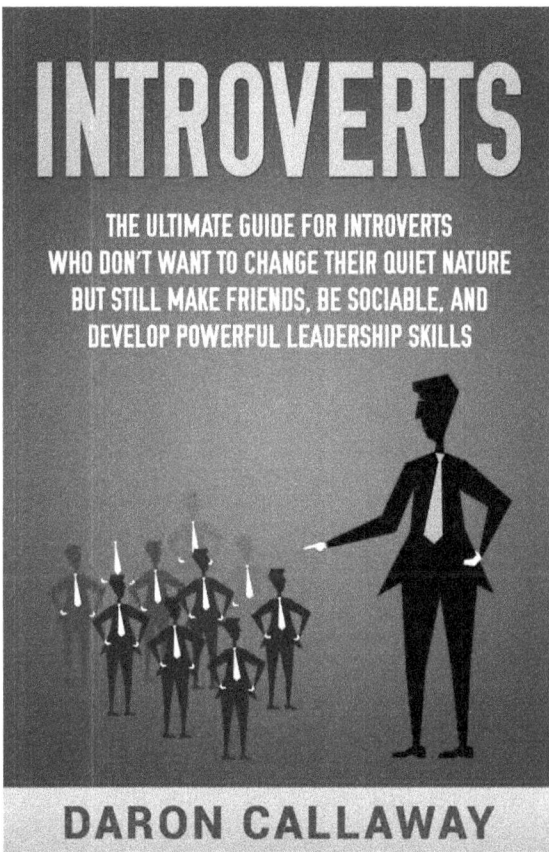

Introduction

Do you feel nervous when you are in a crowd? Do you feel scared when you have to talk to strangers? Do your palms start to get sweaty when you are forced to initiate a conversation? If the answer to any of these questions is affirmative, then don't worry. You are not the only one in this world with these feelings about social interaction.

The world can be divided into two kinds of people: outgoing people who love talking and partying, and those who like to be alone and enjoy silence. The first category of people are extroverts, while the second category of people are introverts. If you have chosen to read this book, you are most likely an introvert.

Introverts can often seem quite confusing, while being an introvert can be a daunting experience. Being an introvert in a world ruled by extroverts can feel strange and awkward. It does not matter whether you are young or old, living as an introvert in an extroverted world is difficult.

Introverts must face new problems every day just because the world is too extrovert oriented. This leads to the development of various professional as well as personal problems. For instance, introverts try to avoid professional meetings just because they happen in large, crowded meeting halls. Introverts avoid meeting new people because they do not like clubs or bars, parties, crowded restaurants, etc.

There are many problems that introverts face in their lives, but these problems are not impossible to solve. In fact, they are quite easy to solve if you know how to do it. You just need to apply yourself, and this book will help you do that.

This book contains a detailed analysis of the psyche of introverts and the problems that they face in their day-to-day lives. It contains information regarding introverts and their professional, social, and personal lives. Along with this, the book contains excellent tips that can help you to accept your introversion and become a healthy, sociable individual.

To appeal to everyone, this book has been written in a simple, lucid, and easy to understand manner. This way, even a beginner can understand the mind and life of an introvert. Being an introvert can be hard, but this book will help make your life easier.

Chapter One: Are You an Introvert?

Introversion is a personality type that is often misjudged and misunderstood. This is due to the quiet attitude of introverts. Their silence is often confused for being arrogant or rude. Many people believe that introverts do not like people. This is obviously a false stereotype.

Introverts do not mind people. It is just that they need to take breaks from society to recharge their social energy. Introverts often find it difficult to connect with others and to engage in small talk. They prefer indulging in meaningful conversations instead.

Many people believe that it is only the introverted who feel like living in solitude, but this is a myth. Many extroverts prefer their own company from time to time. Nowadays, people may even be confused about their personality type, i.e., whether they are an introvert or an extrovert. In this section, let us have a look at some signs that can help you assess whether a person is an introvert or not.

Signs of Being Introverted

- **Small Talk**

Most introverts hate small talk. They tend to avoid circumstances where they might need to indulge in small talk. They do not like discussing random, trivial things such as the weather, trends, etc. Instead, they would rather have a meaningful talk with someone.

- **Overthinking**

A lot of introverts commit the sin of overthinking. This means that a lot of introverts generally overanalyze situations that actually need little analysis.

- **You Like Solitude**

As we mentioned, introverts love solitude. They like spending time with themselves and enjoy activities such as reading, watching movies, writing, listening to music, etc. They would rather spend the weekend alone instead of going to random, noisy parties. Introverts not only like their solitude, but they need it. This is because introverts generally need to recharge their social energy after meeting people.

- **Leadership Qualities**

This might come as a shock to some, but generally, introverts are good leaders. They can not only think deeply but also connect with others on a deeper level. Due to their excellent listening skills, introverts tend to take in everyone's ideas. They like to listen to everyone's plans and point of view instead of being despotic.

- **Networking Issues**

If introverts attend a networking event such as a party or a date, they find it awkward to be there. In parties where you do not know anyone, you may start feeling pressured, stressed, or isolated. Because they do not care for small talk, introverts prefer smaller groups rather than large crowds.

- **Imagination**

Introverts generally possess vivid imaginations. They are creative and like to be ahead of others. The problem that introverts face is expressing their ideas out loud.

- **Phone Talk**

As said above, introverts are not comfortable talking to people on a phone. They would rather text.

- **Center of Attention**

Introverts do not like being the center of attention. They prefer staying on the sidelines, especially in areas where there are a lot of people.

- **You Need Alone Time to Recharge**

Introverts recharge themselves when they are in solitude. They find social events and gatherings exhausting. To recharge themselves, they often escape to silent and serene surroundings.

- **You Are a Good Listener**

Introverts are generally good listeners, because they do not like to impose their ideas and thoughts on other people.

- **Tight-Knit Group**

Introverts generally do not have a lot of friends, but instead perhaps a handful. They tend to be extremely close to these people.

- **Good Observer**

Introverts are generally good observers, and they pay attention to minute details.

- **Anxiety**

Many introverts face anxiety issues. They tend to overanalyze things.

- **Empathetic**

Introverts can not only understand but also relate to the pains of other people. They can understand other people's emotions and can even channel them.

- **Teamwork**

Introverts prefer working alone, but this does not mean that they don't know how to work in teams or groups. They can be excellent leaders if given the opportunity.

- **Creative**

Introverts are generally creative because they have a potent imagination, good observation skills, and emotional sensitivity. They like to look at the world from a different, skillful perspective.

- **Old Soul**

Introverts hate small talk and tend to have more philosophical and deep conversations; therefore, many people call them "old souls."

- **Outgoing Sucks**

Introverts often feel intimidated by outgoing people. They find it difficult to approach and talk to them.

- **Thoughts to Words**

Introverts have a lot of things to say, but they do not know how to say them. They fear misjudgment and being misunderstood. They find it difficult to convey their ideas and thoughts.

- **Sleeping Issues**

Introvert brains are generally overactive. Therefore, introverts do not fall asleep quickly.

- **Crowds are Strange**

Introverts find it difficult to be in a crowd; they tend to feel like they are out of place.

- **People Assume You are Shy**

Introversion does not equal shyness. It is true that introverts do not like socializing a lot, but they are not scared of other people. Shy people find it daunting to socialize with others. And shy extroverts are generally not comfortable being alone most of the time.

- **Initiating Conversations**

Introverts do not like initiating conversations. They find it difficult to start a conversation because they hate small talk. But this does not mean that they do not like talking to people. If someone approaches them, they can generally hold great conversations.

- **Argumentative**

Introverts avoid confrontations and arguments. They do not like snapping at people. They would rather wait and check out the situation before arguing with someone. They like keeping things mellow and quiet.

- **Zoning Out**

Introverts have highly developed brains, and they are creative. Their imagination is quite active. They generally tend to zone out from time to time whenever crowds or loud noises surround them.

Types of Introversion

The media is full of articles, lists, and stories about the difference between introverts and extroverts. While a lot of information is available about introverts, not many people know that there are four types of introverts. There are a lot of differences between personalities, but according to prevalent theory, there exist four types of introversion: social introversion, anxious introversion, thinking introversion, and restrained introversion. Let us have a look at each.

- **Social Introversion**

Social introversion is the most stereotyped and clichéd of all the introversion types. The social introvert prefers to live alone and does not like to interact with other people. He or she prefers solitude and avoids socializing. His or her group of friends (and close family members) is very small and extremely tight knit.

Social introverts generally find their energy in solitude. They would rather be alone than with a group. Groups drain them mentally, emotionally, and even physically.

Social introversion is often confused with shyness; many people believe that social introverts are shy. But just being a social introvert does not make you shy. Social introverts can be quite outgoing, but they prefer solitude to company. Shy people may be quite outgoing, but they are disinclined to join or socialize with groups.

• **Thinking Introversion**

This type of introvert likes to think about going out and talking to others. For him or her, the world would be perfect if it were as they imagine it could be. These introverts like thinking and analyzing ideas. They like to indulge in nostalgia; they prefer getting lost in their memories and thoughts (but not in a neurotic way).

• **Anxious Introversion**

The third type of introversion is anxious introversion. As the name suggests, the people who have this kind of introversion are generally worried and anxious about situations. They like solitude and enjoy being alone. They tend to feel anxious and awkward when they are in a large crowd, often feeling overly self-conscious.

This kind of introversion is generally related to previous social problems encountered in the course of conversations and interactions. Because of those past experiences anxious introverts tend to find it difficult to relate well to other people. But this does not mean that these past experiences cannot be alleviated; the affected introvert's perspectives can be changed to allow them to feel more comfortable in social situations.

Two methods that can help introverts to alleviate the negative impact of these situations are counseling and therapy. With the help of counseling and therapy, you can rebuild your social confidence.

• **Restrained Introversion**

This is an uncommon form of introversion, not seen as often as other forms of introversion. These introverts find it difficult to relate to other people and to "warm up" to others. They like the company of other people, but only after they get used to the people and the situation. These people are generally known as "reserved". They prefer to think before they speak, and to observe other people before they present their ideas.

While these are the four basic types of introversions there are many more. It is impossible to distinguish all forms of introversion, as they are highly intricate and overlapping. This model can help you understand the basic types of introversion and understand yourself better. But do not use these types to pigeonhole yourself. Generally, people tend to have a mixture of all the above four types. Remember, people are complex, and pigeonholing them into one type will always fetch incorrect results.

Famous Introverts

A lot of people believe that to be successful, you need to have an outgoing personality, i.e., you need to be an extrovert. But this is a myth. In fact, a lot of famous people achieved their success because they were (are) introverted. In this section, let us have a look at some of the most successful and well-known introverts.

- **Albert Einstein**

Albert Einstein is perhaps the most famous scientist and physicist in the world. He was also one of the most renowned introverts. Einstein firmly believed that his knowledge, success, and creativity were all a result of his introversion and habit of introspection. He found new ideas and discovered things when he sat down in solitude.

Like Einstein, you can sit in solitude and enjoy the peace. It will help you think creatively about the tasks that you want to do.

- **Bill Gates**

Bill Gates is one of the richest and most successful people in the world. He is also an introvert. He believes that the tranquility and serenity found in solitude can help a person become successful because solitude allows people to think over their ideas patiently, looking at them from all points of view, and combining the ideas thus sorted out with the energy of extroverts can make a company achieve great success.

Another factor that is worth noticing about Gates is that while he is an introvert, he is not shy. This shows that no one is a true introvert (or true extrovert.)

- **Eleanor Roosevelt**

Eleanor Roosevelt was an iconic public figure who will always be remembered for her press conferences, public lectures, and charismatic personality. So, it may come as a surprise to many people that Roosevelt was an introvert. She was of the firm opinion that it is crucial to be friends with yourself, and that if you cannot be your own friend then you cannot be friends with others. To become friends with yourself, you need to enjoy and relax in solitude.

Solitude allows you to be sensitive about other people and their problems. It allows you to relate to people on a different level. Therefore, introversion can help you connect with others through solitude.

- **Meryl Streep**

Actors are often thought to extroverts because they tend to be outgoing, expressive, and have a lot of confidence. But a surprising number of actors are introverts. One of the brightest examples is Meryl Streep. Meryl Streep is a confident and talented actress, but she likes to enjoy her solitude from time to time. She understands her introverted characteristics and uses them to her advantage.

These examples show that introverts are not superior to extroverts, or vice versa. Both types have their strengths and weaknesses, and it depends on how you use them.

So, introverts are unique in their own way, and you do not need to be hard on yourself for being one. You cannot change yourself and become an extrovert. If you believe your introversion is creating problems in your life, you can change the traits slightly, or like Streep, use your introverted characteristics to your advantage.

You need to remember that no one is thoroughly extroverted or introverted. You need to learn how to adapt to the situations or accept them. Use your creativity and passion to lead the world and live your life to the fullest.

Chapter Two: Introvert Myths

As mentioned, there are many myths associated with introverts. A lot of these mythical stereotypes are harmless, but some of them can hurt your integrity and image. In this section, let us have a look at some myths associated with introversion.

"Introverts are Shy"

Many people believe that introverts are shy and that they do not like interacting with others. This is false. Introverts like interacting with people, but they find it draining, and therefore they don't do it often. Shyness is not an introvert-specific trait. Extroverts can be shy as well.

"Introverts Don't Like People"

Introverts like people as much as extroverts do. But instead of approaching everyone and talking to everyone all the time, introverts tend to be reserved and approach people with caution. Introverts prefer intimate meetings to social occasions. They have few friends, but these friends are extremely close.

"Introverts Lack Social Skills"

Introverts are not socially awkward. They tend to have good social skills. Many times, people view some introverts as extroverts because they are adept at social skills.

"Introverts Lack Thoughts and Ideas"

Having ideas and expressing them are two different things. Introverts find it difficult to express their ideas, but this does not mean that they don't get excellent ones. In fact, many well-known geniuses of the world were introverts. The minds of introverts are like locked books. You need to possess the proper keys to open them, but once open, these books are full of hidden treasures and immaculate knowledge. Introverts tend to think a lot before expressing their views and ideas.

"Introverts Love Solitude"

Introverts indeed love solitude, but they do not always want to be solitary and lonely. Introverts crave intimacy just as much as extroverts. They do not like being lonely; there is a difference between being alone and loneliness.

"Introverts Are Boring"

Introverts are not boring, but they tend to get tired while socializing. Introverts know how to enjoy parties, but they do not like them too much. Introverts can dance, sing, travel, and have fun, too.

"Introverts Are Depressed"

Introverts are not depressed. Introverts like being alone, but this desire is not a sign of depression. The desire to be alone rises out of their desire to restore their energy via quiet time. It is their time to refuel.

"Introverts Are a Minority"

While it is true that there are more extroverted people in this world than introverts, introverts form around 30-40% of the total population.

"Introverts Like Listening, not Speaking"

It is true that introverts are generally great listeners, but this does not mean that they do not like to speak. Introverts enjoy speaking, but they need to be invited to do so. If they are drained, then they prefer listening over speaking.

"Introverts Can't Stand Being Interrupted"

Like every other person, introverts find it exceptionally rude and frustrating when someone constantly interrupts them. When this happens and introverts pause, it does not mean that they have nothing to say; they are just collecting their thoughts.

"Introverts Don't Like Conversations"

Introverts do not like small talk. They do not like to indulge in social pleasantries because they tire of them quickly. Introverts do not like talking on the phone. Unfortunately, disinterest in these activities is often considered to be rude by extroverts. This is because extroverts primarily designed the rules and etiquettes of socializing. While introverts try to be as polite as possible, sometimes it becomes too difficult.

"Introverts Like Loneliness"

The fact that introverts need "me" time is well known. Still, many people feel offended when introverts excuse themselves to be alone. Extroverts often believe that introverts are rude and that they do not like the extrovert, which is why they try to excuse themselves. Instead of taking things personally, extroverts should try to understand the mindset and needs of introverts.

"Introversion Can Be Cured"

This is an extremely offensive myth because it perpetuates the false notion that there is something wrong with introversion, and that it is a disease. Introverts cannot be cured because they are not suffering from any disease. Introverts are perfectly natural.

"Introverts are Judgmental"

Introverts like being silent, causing some people to think that they are judgmental. Introverts tend to think and reflect upon subjects before speaking. Some of them even daydream while being silent. Silence should not be confused with being judgmental.

"Introverts Lack Emotions"

Introverts are not unemotional. They feel all the emotions that extroverts feel, but they express them in a milder form. The feelings, emotions, and expressions of introverts are reserved and inhibited compared to those of extroverts. They do not like to wear their hearts on their sleeves. Introverts share their feelings only with their true friends and people whom they trust.

Chapter Three: Understanding Introverted Personalities

Introversion can be quite confusing, even for introverts themselves. In this chapter, let us have a closer look at introversion and various aspects of introversion.

MBTI

The MBTI or the Myers-Briggs Type Indicator test is a personality test based on the theories of Carl Jung, that divides people into 16 categories. According to this theory, all individuals act in particular ways which can help researchers to divide them into specific categories. People who fall into certain categories display the characteristics of these categories.

The 16 categories are equally divided into introverted categories and extroverted categories. In this section, let us have a look at the introverted personality types.

Personality Types

As explained in the previous chapter, introverted individuals like to indulge in solitude. They prefer thinking things over before they take any action. Many times, introverts are too focused on the idea and the thought processes instead of action. Therefore, many introverts prefer the "idea" of something over the "real thing" itself.

Let us now have a look at the eight MBTI introverted personalities.

- **ISTJ**

Introverted / Sensing / Thinking / Judging

ISTJs are serious, strong, peaceful, and quiet. They prefer the serene beauty of life. If you are an ISTJ individual, you are most likely dependable, responsible, and thorough. Individuals who are ISTJs are highly practical and logical. They are focused and work hard to reach their goals. Sometimes they can be quite the traditionalists. They prefer order over chaos and keep their surroundings as organized as possible.

- **ISFJ**

Introverted / Sensing / Feeling / Judging

These individuals are kind, quiet, and conscientious. They are well-known for being responsible. They like to commit to things and follow through on them. They often put the needs of other people above their own. They are practical and like stability. They are attuned to the feelings of other people, and like helping others.

- **INFJ**

Introverted / Intuitive / Feeling / Judging

INFJs are sensitive, forceful, and original but in a quiet and reserved way. They like to find the meaning of connections between ideas, people, and possessions. They are highly curious. They work hard to understand the motives of other people. They are firm about their decisions and values. They possess clarity of ideas and thoughts. They know how to achieve the common good. They are organized, which helps them implement their clear ideas properly.

- **INTJ**

Introverted / Intuitive / Thinking / Judging

INTJs are supposed to be analytical, independent, determined, and original. They can turn ideas into action. They can detect patterns in external events. When they are committed to things, they will see them through. INTJ individuals have high standards and like to judge their own performance as critically as they do that of others. They have excellent leadership qualities, but they can also work under existing leaders.

- **ISTP**

Introverted / Sensing / Thinking / Perceiving

These individuals are generally reserved and quiet. They like to observe things to understand their workings. They are skilled in mechanical work. Many of these individuals are interested in extreme sports and excel at them. These individuals are tolerant and flexible. Instead of jumping to conclusions immediately, they think things over and observe them from a distance until the solution becomes apparent. Some people find these individuals detached and excessively practical, but their practicality helps them easily find solutions to complex problems.

- **ISFP**

Introverted / Sensing / Feeling / Perceiving

ISFP means one who is kind, quiet, sensitive, and serious. They do not like conflict and rarely engage in things that can lead to disagreements. They are faithful and loyal. They are open-minded and extremely flexible. They are generally creative and original. They like to do work by taking their own time. They appreciate the present and enjoy experiencing it.

- **INFP**

Introverted / Intuitive / Feeling / Perceiving

INFPs are extremely sensitive about their values, and they stay loyal to people whom they admire. They are quiet, reflective, and are often thought to be idealistic. They generally have a highly developed personal-value system, and rarely go against it. They are adaptable, loyal, and laid back, but their laid-back nature disappears as soon as one of their values gets threatened.

- **INTP**

Introverted / Intuitive / Thinking / Perceiving

INTPs are known to be creative, original, and logical. They like theories and ideas and get excited about them. They prefer knowledge, logic, and competence over other aspects. They are reserved and like to be quiet, which is why they often appear to be mysterious. They are lone wolves and do not like following or leading others.

It is clear from all this that there are different types of introverts present in this world. Many people tend to identify with multiple MBTI types. All these types have their own strengths and weaknesses, and none of them is stronger (or weaker) than the others.

Chapter Four: What Does It Feel Like to Be an Introvert?

If you are reading this book, you are either an introvert or an extrovert who is trying to understand the intricacies of introversion. Either way, it is necessary to understand how introverts generally feel. Even introverts sometimes find it difficult to understand their feelings. Dealing with the hardships of life as an introvert can be quite daunting.

Not everyone understands what it feels like to be an introverted person. The world is indeed changing rapidly, and now people have become more accepting, but introverts still form a minority. According to some researchers, only 30% of the total population is introverted. A lot of misconceptions are present about introverts, including a lot of stereotypes and myths. These stereotypes are often so farfetched that they miss the mark totally.

For instance, many people have the misconception that introverts are lonely and shy. They feel that introverts are generally afraid of other people. This, of course, is false. Being an introvert is just like being an extrovert; the experiences are similar but are processed differently.

Being an introvert is no different in this regard than being an extrovert or an ambivert. Many introverts share the same hobbies and activities that extroverts or ambiverts enjoy. These include parties and talking to friends. But there exist some differences in the level of emotions between the two. One of the biggest differences between introverts and extroverts is how they regard solitude.

All individuals need "social energy" to interact with others. Extroverts are like powerhouses of social energy because they receive social energy by being sociable. But introverts cannot do this. Their energy is only recharged when they are alone and solitary. This is why being introverted can often be exhausting.

Introverts like Being Alone

Introverts love being alone. For introverts, solitude does not equal emptiness, boredom, or loneliness. They feel extremely comfortable when alone. They like thinking on their own and pondering things. They enjoy solo activities such as origami, art, drawing, reading, etc. Introverts do not consider solitude "filler time"; for an introvert, solitude is the best time of the day.

If you are an introvert, finding "me time" in today's world can be quite difficult. Finding a quiet and solitary time without interruptions has become difficult. If introverts do not get their "me" time, they may become snappy and frustrated. They need their time to contemplate, like monks, else they find the world too much to handle.

While introverts enjoy their solitude and like spending time with themselves, this does not mean that they do not enjoy the company of other people. Many introverts recharge their social energy by being solitary and then use this energy to interact with each other. Introverts are, after all, human beings, and human beings are social animals. They cannot live without the company of others. They want to interact with others after their "me" time. But the duration of this "me" time differs from individual to individual.

Introverts and Socializing

Extroverts find "alone time" scary and boring. Some extroverts get extremely restless when they are alone for too long. Extroverts feel happy when they are with people; they try to be in the company of other people as much as possible.

For introverts, socializing means a totally different thing. They either do not enjoy it as much as extroverts, or they enjoy it but find it absolutely exhausting.

Certain activities, places, and situations are more tiring than others for introverts. For instance, introverts find large crowds more tiring than smaller ones; they find noisy places more tiring than quiet ones. They find talking to strangers more difficult than talking to people they know.

All social activities wear out introverts. They may enjoy it thoroughly, but they will get quite tired compared to extroverts at the same affair. But this does not mean that there is anything wrong with them. It is just the way they are wired. If you are an introvert, then enjoy your introversion and solitude.

The Effects of Dopamine

Being an introvert is genetic. There is a significant difference between the brains of introverts and extroverts; their brains handle dopamine in different ways. Dopamine is the "reward chemical" of the brain; it is a neurotransmitter that brings in the feeling of ecstasy.

How Dopamine Affects Extroverts

The brains of extroverts are less sensitive to dopamine. This means that they need a lot of outside stimulation to feel happy and energized. Therefore, they tend to enjoy talking, chatting, laughing, smiling, dancing, and spending time with people. They like to keep themselves active and busy.

The brains of introverts are far more sensitive to dopamine as compared to extroverts. They feel satisfied and rewarded quickly. They do not need a lot of stimuli. Therefore, introverts enjoy sitting in solitude and thinking things over, and enjoy spending quiet time with their books. An excessively loud environment like a large crowd will overstimulate the brains of introverts, causing them to tire quickly.

Loud and noisy environments are draining experiences for introverts as well as extroverts. But introverts find it much more draining than extroverts. Extroverts continue to enjoy loud environments because it gives them dopamine. Therefore, they continue to dance, chat, or talk to people.

Chapter Five: Introverts and Quiet Time

Why Do Introverts Love Being Alone?

If you are an introvert, you probably love being alone at times. You probably prefer sitting alone, reading, and thinking to partying all day. You would rather indulge in a thought-provoking conversation than shallow small talk. You prefer spending time alone. A popular meme targeting introverts say that there is nothing better in the world (for introverts) than when their friends cancel plans.

Introverts like and, in fact, *need* alone time because if they don't get it, they become mentally drained. Introverts regain their energy through solitude. If they do not get some solitary time, they tend to get drained mentally and emotionally. They become frustrated, and every little problem and annoyance becomes gigantic for them. They stop functioning properly, their thinking suffers, and even a little annoyance can make them immensely angry or sad. If the situation continues, then they may become physically exhausted or may even fall sick.

All the above things are common all over the world. But these things happen not because introverts are inherently cranky and evil. There are a lot of scientific reasons behind how people act and behave. Dopamine plays an integral role in deciding how we behave in day-to-day life.

Introverts, Extroverts, and Rewards

We do things so that the brain can get enough or, better still, ample amounts of dopamine. As we discussed earlier, extroverts need a lot of dopamine to feel satisfaction and happiness, while the brains of introverts become satiated with little servings. Therefore, many times, the rewards that can motivate and excite extroverts can also tire them.

- **Introverts Don't Need as Much Stimulation**

All this can be boiled down to the simple fact that introverts do not require a lot of stimulation to feel rewarded. The level of stimulation that extroverts enjoy is often too much for introverts. For instance, extroverts love parties because they involve a lot of stimulation, like a lot of people talking together, the chaos, the loud music, lights, crowd, alcohol, etc. For extroverts, this is heaven, but for introverts it's not so heavenly for long. This is because the brains of introverts will get overstimulated, and they will find it difficult to focus anywhere. If you are an introvert caught in a party like this, it is better to escape, go back home, and enjoy a simple dinner while watching TV. It will help you reduce the overstimulation and will make you feel calm and happy once again.

- **The Dopamine Difference**

In the last chapter, we saw how introverts do not care about rewards as much as extroverts do. This is because their tolerance of a neurotransmitter called dopamine. Dopamine is present in our brains, and it is often known as the "reward chemical" or "feel-good" chemical. This is because dopamine is responsible for the reward and pleasure centers of the brain.

Many people believe that socializing is only tiring for introverts, but this is not true. Extroverts feel tired after a lot of socializing as well. Dopamine can help you reduce this stress. But what makes introverts and extroverts different is that dopamine helps extroverts a lot while socializing because it gives them energy boosts from time to time. Extroverts are born with an active dopamine system. Introverts are not blessed with a strong dopamine system, and they feel tired mentally as well as physically after socializing.

Extroverts and People

Extroverts also prefer being with people more than introverts because extroverts place a lot of significance on people. According to a recent study, it was found that extroverts feel highly stimulated when they see and meet new people. Introverts, on the other hand, pay more attention to inanimate objects.

Chapter Six: The Comfort Zone Myth

Everyone believes that if a person wants to succeed, he or she needs to get out of his or her comfort zone. But most of the time, people only say this to introverts. And when they say this, they mean "Become more like extroverts if you want to succeed." This is why that, while it sounds meaningful and important, "comfort zone" is such a loaded and oftentimes problematic term.

Due to the prevalence of this statement, a lot of introverts try to "break out of their shell." They try hard to get out of their "comfort zone." Not only is this a difficult (and perhaps impossible) task, but it is also a harrowing and painful experience. Almost no introvert succeeds in doing this because an introvert can't become an extrovert, nor vice versa. The only thing an introvert can do is become a fake extrovert. But it is an unsustainable decision that takes its toll.

If you, being an introvert, try to get out of your "comfort zone" you will start copying the extroverts around you. Each person and personality type are born with certain assets. For instance, introverts are born with good listening and observation skills. They think and analyze things before making decisions. But when you try to come out of your "comfort zone," you start forgoing these skills and replacing them with pseudo-extrovert characteristics. But adopting the strength of another personality type is not simple. You cannot take over these skills and hope for the best. You may even lose your own assets while trying to gain these new ones. Ultimately, it is far better to play to your strengths instead of changing things around all the time.

What is a Comfort Zone?

As said above, the comfort zone is a loaded term with a lot of meanings and definitions. But in simple words, the comfort zone includes situations, people, skillsets, and places in which a person feels comfortable, competent, and safe. It includes all the circumstances that you find enjoyable and pleasing. The edge of the comfort zone is a confusing place. It is as if you have one foot in the "uncomfortable zone" and one foot in the "comfort zone." People generally find this zone more complex and challenging than their comfort zone. While you can handle situations in this zone without too much anxiety and other such problems, it is still much more difficult than the comfort zone. Anything beyond this zone is considered to be "out of your comfort zone."

But this is a shallow understanding of the comfort zone concept, because situations that need a lot of talking, robust actions, and interactions are the extroverts' comfort zone. As explained in the previous chapter, the brains of extroverts and introverts handle dopamine differently. Extroverts feel comfortable and happy when exciting things surround them. They are wired like that. They like to jump into the action right away. They don't get tired from meeting new people, and they enjoy the hustle and bustle of the world. This is why extroverts feel comfortable while visiting large meetings, parties, and conventions. As a lot of people in this world are extroverts, most of the social conventions are designed to accommodate them. Therefore, introverts are forced to get out of their comfort zone and enter the comfort zones of extroverts. This is a discriminating situation because introverts will never succeed in tackling these environments because introverts will always be the outsiders in the comfort zones of extroverts.

Extroverts exhibit being comfortable on the outside, but introverts feel comfortable on the inside. The comfort zone of introverts is inside their mind. They feel comfortable in situations that require a lot of planning, thinking, and precision. This is because their nervous system is wired that way. They prefer to rest and understand things properly before making decisions. If introverts do not get their alone time to reflect and introspect, they feel drained. They find large and noisy crowds overwhelming. Their thinking clouds in such situations. This is why introverts tend to avoid the spotlight.

Unlike extroverts, introverts find solace and comfort in small gatherings, quiet places, and in solitude. They do not feel comfortable with strangers and would rather talk to the people they know. They do not need a lot of outside stimuli. Instead, they prefer the calmness and soothing sounds of nature.

But, as we have seen, the extroverts run the world (allegedly), and they decide the rules, which is why introverts are often forced to come out of their comfort zones and enter the zones of extroverts. Many researchers believe that, like extroverts, if introverts can work while being in their own comfort zone, it can work wonders toward making the endeavors more successful.

Complacent Zone

When people tell introverts (and extroverts, too) to come out of their comfort zone, they mean the complacency zone. The complacency zone is different from the comfort zone, and it would be nice if everyone started using the term "complacency zone" instead of "comfort zone". The term comfort zone now has many negative connotations, and it's better to avoid the term altogether.

Everyone needs to get out of their complacency zone if they want to succeed. The complacency zone is the zone in which we tend to seek shelter from the problems of the world. This zone allows us to maintain a false status quo which helps us feel safe. But safety hinders your progress. You cannot grow if you do not take risks and remain hiding in a safe house most of the time. The complacency zone only provides you with a false sense of security and safety. It is false because it only leads to failure and stagnation. You will get stuck in a place or position if you don't take risks.

When a person is in the complacency zone, he or she will try to invoke a variety of rationales to justify his or her presence in the zone. If you ever want to succeed, you need to start listening to your inner voice. If it's making excuses for you constantly occupying your complacency zone, it may be time for some adjustments.

Working from the Comfort Zone

Almost all extroverts work from their comfort zone, while introverts are often forced out of theirs. Pulling a crab out of its shell kills it; pulling an introvert out of his or her comfort zone hinders his or her abilities significantly. Once introverts understand that they can perform their best while being in their comfort zone, they will never want to come out of it. This is excellent because their comfort zone will allow them to be free, excited, creative, and enthusiastic.

But remember, do not confuse your comfort zone with your complacency zone. You need to get out of your complacency zone but stay in your comfort zone. This will help you to move forward in your personal and professional life.

Chapter Seven: Introverts and Mental Health

Mental Issues Faced by Introverts and Extroverts

Mental health is a complex topic. Whether introvert or extrovert, mental health issues can plague anyone. Both personality types need to pay close attention to their mental health.

As said in the previous chapter, introverts are often considered shy because they like solitude and spending time with themselves. But excessive isolation can lead to the development of a lot of problems. Excessive isolation is a sign of depression and many other mental health issues.

Extroverts generally like to spend a lot of time surrounded by people. But an overdose of this can turn an individual into an excessively clingy person. Both personality types face their own problems.

Introverts especially should stay cautious. They can often become too isolated. There is a huge difference between solitude and loneliness. If you constantly isolate yourself from other people, it can lead to the development of various mental diseases and disorders such as social anxiety and depression. In fact, excessive isolation is a potent symptom of depression. If you feel that you like isolation too much, then you should check whether your need for isolation is a result of a lack of energy or has some other serious underlying cause. Other serious mental disorders that can lead to (and arise from) excessive isolation include addictions, personality problems, and eating disorders. An introverted person should always have a strong support system consisting of people whom they can trust. If you are an introvert who likes solitude a lot, talk to your friends and try to form a group that can keep a check on you. If you do not have close friends with whom you can share your emotions and vulnerable thoughts, then it is time to find some.

You also need to establish whether you are really an introvert or not. Sometimes people get introversion confused with social and anxiety-related disorders.

A personal assessment is crucial to avoid problems in this area; if you believe that your discomfort is a result of social anxiety, then it is recommended you contact a therapist or a mental health professional as soon as possible.

While isolation is the major problem related to introversion, many other problems can become serious as well. Introverts are generally more susceptible to depression than extroverts. Neurological studies have proven that the brain activity of introverts is stronger and more intense than the brain activity in extroverts. This is why introverts do not need as many stimuli as extroverts. Having an active brain is a great thing because it allows introverts to be creative, thoughtful, and innovative. But an overactive brain can lead to various other problems. For instance, if you have an overactive brain, you will tend to overthink a lot, leaving you feeling overwhelmed. It is also bad for people who tend to get over-emotional. Overthinking is especially bad if you obsess over negative ideas and thoughts. This problem becomes even more severe when the person is secluded and prefers living in isolation. Seclusion bottles up these emotions of pain and despair, and this bottling up results in the development of feelings such as hopelessness, shame, guilt, helplessness, and worthlessness. These feelings act as a gateway to more severe mental health issues.

Ultimately, there is nothing wrong with being an extrovert or an introvert. Both have their particular characteristics, and both of them have their pros and cons. Both personality types share the same mental health problems. Mental health issues should not be taken as a sign of weakness. Mental disorders are just like any other disorder. You just need to check for the symptoms from time to time. If you believe that you have symptoms of any mental health disorder, it is recommended you contact a health professional as soon as possible.

Why Should Introverts Have a Health Plan?

Introverts love quiet time. Whenever they are in solitude, introverts tend to be more productive and reliable. They tend to get brilliant ideas when they are left alone. They can accomplish a lot of things if they are allowed to have their time, silence, and space. But solitude can be a curse as well. If introverts live in solitude a lot, their minds can take over and start thinking negatively. This can lead to the development of various psychological issues. Many times, introverts become overwhelmed because they cannot control their psychological problems and negative ideas. Additionally, the typical Introverts' creativity intensifies the problem.

This phenomenon is seen in many introverts all over the world. It can lead to the development of a mental crisis which can be quite difficult to deal with. So, there are certain mental health precautions that every introvert must take. If you, as an introvert, do not have a medical emergency plan, you may end up in a psychiatric ward. In this section, let us have a look at why you should always have a proper mental health plan in place.

• **Introverts and Expanded Psychiatric Services**

Introverts need to have an emergency mental health plan because they are more likely than extroverts to face a mental health emergency. In 2010 two researchers, Laurie Helgoe and Nancy Ancowitz, came up with an article suggesting that the American Psychological Association should include introversion as a significant factor in the diagnosis of personality disorders. Introverts spend a lot of time thinking; if the thoughts are positive, it does not matter much, but if their mind is full of negative thoughts, it can overwhelm them. They may become antisocial. In some extreme cases, people have become agoraphobic. These and many other related problems can lead to the development of mental health emergencies. Introverts must study the signs and symptoms of the most common mental disorders. Along with knowing these symptoms, they should also have an action plan that can help in tackling mental health emergencies.

- **Emergency Psych Services (U.S.) and Silence**

The psych services available in the United States of America are not introvert friendly. These services are rarely private or quiet. As introverts require their share of peace and seclusion every day, a noisy and excessively public place can aggravate their symptoms. Instead of helping, these services can often exacerbate problems.

This is why many introverts avoid getting help for their problems; they are worried about the environment in which they will have to live. But various options can help you avoid this environment and still get treatment. For instance, if the problem is not too severe, you can leave the place after spending a night. If you set up these things before the problem arises, you will have everything planned, and you will not be left at the mercy of the staff. Some new psych services consider the needs and requirements of introverts and try to provide a friendly and comfortable atmosphere for them. Try to locate a service like this near you. If you cannot find one, then use the "overnighter" option.

- **Introverts and a Tiny Social Circle**

One of the biggest differences between introverts and extroverts is their social circle. Extroverts tend to have a large social circle. This way, if ever an emergency or crisis arises, they can have a lot of friends who can help them, and their friends will call other people to help.

This is not feasible in the case of introverts. Introverts generally have a small social circle. They do not have a lot of friends. While the quantity of relationships for introverts is low, the quality is exceptionally good. This is because introverts tend to spend a lot of time with the same people, which results in the development of stronger relationships, attachments, and connections. This is why you need to make your friends aware of your problems. You need to choose your contacts carefully so that they can rush to help you. If you are in a mental health emergency situation, you will be confused and will not understand what to do. It is therefore recommended that you let your friends know about your problem beforehand so that if an emergency comes up, they will have control over the situation.

- **Introverts and Ignoring Health Problems**

It is a well-known fact that introverts are private individuals who do not like talking a lot about themselves. They love being left to their own devices, which is why many introverts avoid going to their doctors regularly. This is because doctors tend to ask a lot of questions of the patients. Introverts do not particularly like answering questions about their personal life, especially if there is nothing wrong with them. But that's how doctors work. This is why you need to have a regular mental as well as physical checkup to avoid any surprise diseases and disorders. A regular mental health checkup will help you avoid a sudden anxiety attack or will at least keep you prepared for one.

- **Preventing Attacks**

If you are an introvert, you may feel overwhelmed from time to time. You may also feel that your emotions are holding you back. But this does not mean that you cannot live a healthy and fulfilling life. Introverts often feel lost, especially in cases such as anxiety attacks and panic attacks. While that is not the case with all introverts, everyone needs to have a plan to keep things under control. This will help prevent a full-blown panic or anxiety attack. Remember that knowledge is power.

If you feel that you may fall prey to a mental health problem in the future, you should be vigilant at all times. You need to care for yourself and your mental health. Let us have a look at some tips that can help you keep your mind sound and sharp.

Professional Advice

Everyone visits a dentist or a physician for annual checkups; you should form a habit of visiting a mental health professional to get yourself checked out from time to time. It is true that this is a costly affair, but if money is not an issue for you, then you can find a decent psychiatrist or psychologist who can help you immensely.

If money is an issue, then check whether your insurance covers mental health professionals. This will allow you to get help at a low cost.

If your insurance does not cover mental health, then try seeking other options such as public assistance.

If you ever feel inclined to cause yourself harm, call 911 in the U.S. (999 in the U.K.) as soon as possible. Remember, your life is more important than money.

Know Yourself

Introverts love seclusion, and they spend a lot of time alone. This is why, when something goes wrong with them, people around them rarely notice it. If you tend to spend a lot of time alone, then you need to know yourself properly. This means you should be able to understand yourself and your general behavior patterns. If you ever begin acting differently, you will notice the change quickly.

Emergencies and Non-Emergencies

You need to have a proper plan related to emergencies and non-emergencies. You should know where to go or whom to meet if emergency situations arise. For instance, if you have a mental health emergency, you may find it difficult to think clearly, so know beforehand which friend(s) you should contact as soon as possible. Dealing with a worst-case scenario can be easier if you have the best plan ready.

Making a mental health plan takes a lot of time and effort, but in the end, it is worth it. Instead of wasting a lot of money and time later, it is better to put in some effort now.

Caution

The suggestions given in this chapter are precautionary. Do not consider them medical recommendations. You should always talk to a medical professional before changing your routine drastically. And do not self-medicate.

Chapter Eight: 15 Ways to Increase Happiness as an Introvert

If you feel bad about being an introvert, don't worry; you are not alone. Many introverts wish that they could be more like their extroverted peers. Extroverts do not feel mentally and physically drained after meeting or socializing with people.

But as you now know, introversion is perfectly natural; there is nothing wrong with being an introvert. The only problem that you may face frequently is how to be happy in an extroverted world. But don't worry; this chapter contains brilliant tips that can help you be content and stay happy.

Time is Essential

Introverts need a lot of time to recover after attending networking events and parties; they also need time to recover after doing ordinary things like shopping in a crowded place, enjoying a heated discussion, or having a stressful day at work. After such occasions, introverts need some time to think and recover. This unwinding time is necessary as it allows them to calm down and relax. If introverts do not get their "me" time, they feel tired, unwell, and "brain-dead".

Meaningful Conversation

Introverts do not care for meaningless conversation; they feel uncomfortable when someone tries making small talk with them. Many introverts learn the art of small talk, but they nonetheless perform it with mild discomfort. Most introverts do not like talking, but if you are one of those who do, try to find partners with whom you can have meaningful conversations. Meaningful conversations will keep you happy and contented.

But don't worry, meaningful conversations do not mean that you need to ask each other soul-searching questions all the time. Sometimes you may feel like talking about random things such as what your partner did over the weekend. This doesn't mean that you care much for small talk; you still need a meaningful conversation from time to time to keep you afloat.

Companionable Silence

While this point may counter the last one, it is true. As an introvert, you need some quiet "me" time now and then. If you are comfortable with a person, you can enjoy sitting next to them while saying nothing. Introverts do not mind if there are a lot of pauses in a conversation; silence is golden for introverts.

Hobbies and Interests

Introverts generally have many hobbies. Many introverts are highly interested in gardening, reading, cooking, painting, writing, mythology, etc. Introverts generally like to delve deep into their hobbies. Hobbies are a great way to recharge energy.

A Quiet Space

Every introvert likes to have a quiet sanctuary in his or her house. They need a quiet, private space to get away from the hustle and bustle of life. If you have such a room in your house, decorate it according to your whims. In this room, you should feel comfortable and happy. There should not be frequent interruptions in this room.

Time to Think

Introverts need time to think. According to Dr. Laney, introverts use their long-term memory more than their working memory. This is the opposite of extroverts. Many introverts find it difficult to express themselves because they need some time to think over things before expressing them. If introverts are not allowed to think over things before speaking, they may find the situation uncomfortable.

Friends Who Understand

Introverts do not mind socializing, but they need it to happen on their terms. Introverts love their friends, but they prefer people who can let them be themselves.

Work

Instead of working just for money, introverts will always prefer a career that they can enjoy. Introverts are rarely content with something that does not satisfy them intellectually. Introverts crave work, and they want their lives to have a purpose. They don't want a job that pays them well but does not satisfy those other needs.

Permission to Remain Silent

Introverts prefer to stay silent rather than talk. You must have felt like this before; sometimes you do not want to interact with someone because you just do not have the energy to do so. But people rarely let introverts be themselves. If you have understanding friends, they will accept that you need to stay silent from time to time.

Independence

Introverts like being independent and unique. They prefer to do things on their own terms. Introverts feel the happiest and most satisfied when they are allowed to work according to their terms. Introverts like to be self-dependent, independent, and self-reliant.

The Simple Life

Introverts like to lead simple lives. They like situations where they can care for others. They need significance in their life; they do not like living a life that has no meaning.

Friends and Loved Ones

Everyone needs people in their life who can understand and accept them despite their foibles and quirks. Introverts do not like being the center of attention, which is why they struggle in large groups. Many times, they disappear in large crowds because they like to hide in a corner. Introverts want nothing more than having a few good friends who understand them and care for them. Introverts know that they can be difficult to "grok" sometimes, but if their friends understand this and still stick with them, they will be the happiest people in the world.

See Your Whole Self

It bears repeating that no one is totally introverted or extroverted. Personality is a broad spectrum, and everyone has some characteristics of introversion as well as extroversion. People who are totally (or even strongly) introverted or extroverted are rare. Most of the people around us fall somewhere towards the middle of this spectrum. This means that people like to socialize sometimes, and sometimes they tend to avoid crowds and prefer to sit alone instead. If a person lies very near the middle of this spectrum, such people are known as *ambiverts.*

All of us are born with the capability to recharge ourselves through social gatherings, interactions, and affiliation; everyone has some tendency to recharge their energy through solitude and serenity. It is thus necessary to be as honest as possible with yourself. If you feel that you just want to sit alone and talk to no one, do it. If you want to go out and have a talk with a friend or go to a party, then do it. Ultimately, you should do whatever makes you feel happy.

Embrace Your Strengths

Each personality type is born with its own unique strengths. Introverted behavior has a lot of positives. For instance, introverts are often better at solving problems and thinking. They tend to be well-behaved and perform tasks well. They are generally academically gifted. They like taking risks, but they usually only take risks that won't backfire.

According to research, introverts have a lot of gray matter in their prefrontal cortex. This area is present in the front area of the brain. It controls things such as abstract thinking, complex emotions, and decision-making. This is why introverts are blessed with good thinking powers.

In many theological, philosophical, and classical schools of thought, true happiness is said to be derived from spending time alone in contemplation. Ancient thinkers, from Buddha to Aristotle, popularized this notion. Introverts are already blessed with an inclination toward this truism, as they tend to naturally find solace in solitude. Instead of hiding your introvert characteristics, accept them and celebrate them.

Act the Part

According to research, when introverts come face to face with extroverts, they tend to monitor their behavior and try to act like extroverts. This is due to the social pressure to appear positive and accepting. But this experience is quite uncomfortable for the introvert, who feels they need to fake things and be on their toes at all times. According to this research, if introverts act like themselves without any pressure to be someone they are not, they can be happier. (This obviously pretty much applies to every personality group.)

These are some of the methods that can help you to be happy and stay happy as an introvert. Try them for yourself and adopt the ones that work for you.

Chapter Nine: Conquering Introvert Fears and Phobias

One of the biggest problems that an introvert must face is having to deal with fear and nervousness. According to research, an introverted brain generally tries to find security and safety, which is why even the smallest dangers can make your brain hyperactive. Introverted brains are more sensitive to strong feelings, as they concentrate more on inner sensations. This is why introverts feel fear deeply.

Many people think fear is bad and that it is a highly negative sensation. But this is not true; it is not inherently negative. Like every feeling, it is a reaction to the stimulation received from the outside world or the inside workings. The problem with fear begins when it starts to become excessive. When you start to obsess with fear, it usually interferes with your crucial tasks. That's why introverts often freeze up while socializing.

According to some researchers, human beings are born with only two fears: darkness and loud noises. All the other phobias and fears that we tend to have are later developments. No one is free of fear; everyone is afraid of something. Many introverts are generally shy and socially anxious; these two are forms of fear. If you have these fears, then this chapter will help you overcome them. Let us have a look at some tips and methods that can be used to tackle fear.

Small Talk

There are very few introverts in this world who like small talk. The majority of introverts feel uncomfortable making small talk. Introverts generally hate idle conversation; they find it pointless, which is why they tend to become nervous and start fidgeting.

Many introverts try to indulge in small talk by planning it extensively in their minds, but when they try to express themselves, their mouths go dry and their minds go blank. Introverts do not mind talking as a concept; in fact, many introverts love talking about things that really matter or the things that they find interesting. Introverts prefer chats that can help them connect with the situation or the person in a deeper way.

If you are an introvert who is often called "quiet" or "reserved," it is not because you are shy but because you do not find small talk to be interesting. You find it unimportant and irrelevant. You would rather use your energy in some other endeavor instead of wasting it on small talk.

Meeting New People

Many times, introverts feel scared and nervous when meeting and interacting with strangers. Meeting new people is a great way to make new contacts, but it can be quite a task for introverts. Introverts find the initial stages of any relationship (not just romantic ones) quite difficult.

Introverts are especially uncomfortable in large groups and crowds, and they find it difficult to talk to someone while they are in a crowd. If you feel nervous about introducing yourself to someone, don't worry; just try to relax. If you prefer meeting and interacting with people one on one, don't worry; you are not the only one. Many introverts prefer private conversations to overcrowded interactions. No wonder many introverts find starting new jobs difficult.

Big Crowds

Introverts tend to avoid big crowds but sometimes it is impossible to do so. If you are afraid of meeting strangers, then it is likely that you will be afraid of large crowds as well. A crowd of strangers can be particularly troublesome for introverts who suffer from anxiety problems. As said above, introverts generally gain social and personal energy from solitude; crowds drain their energy quickly. Introverts prefer talking and interacting in small groups. If you find yourself caught in a crowd, try to encircle yourself with your friends. This will make you feel slightly more comfortable and may prevent a panic attack.

Talking on The Phone

If you do not like talking on the phone and get nervous when answering it, then don't worry; you are not alone. In fact, this problem is so common that there is a proper term for it, called *telephonophobia*. Some introverts dislike phone calls altogether, but some find only strangers' calls problematic. Some introverts do not find receiving calls troublesome, but they become immensely nervous when they are asked to initiate a call. Some introverts tend to avoid calls from unknown numbers.

There is no particular reason why you may find phone calls difficult and nerve-wracking. Some people believe it is because you cannot see the person with whom you are talking, and so you cannot study his or her body language. This dissociation between the voice and the body can be quite unsettling to many. Introverts are well known for their skills of observation, so when they are forced to speak on the phone, that skill cannot be employed; this may make them panic.

Long Social Engagements

People often try to coax introverts to parties and similar social events by promising them that it will be fun. "Fun" is a subjective term that changes meaning from individual to individual. Thus, what is fun for an extrovert may not be fun for an introvert. In fact, it may be the opposite of fun for him or her.

Introverts love having a good time with their friends, but they would rather do it on their own terms. They dislike wasting their time at parties, especially if they are long and time-consuming parties. These parties are boring to an introvert and can be quite stressful. If you dislike these activities, it is better to let your friends know about your views. If your friends truly love you, they will try to understand your problem.

Embarrassment

Your introversion will definitely play an integral role in your fear of humiliation. Introverts generally spend a lot of time listening and observing. They usually tend to avoid other people because they don't want to be seen or heard doing something that people will remember negatively. Introverts are highly intuitive. This intuition makes them think of a lot of scenarios about the future and things that may or may not take place. Many times, this speculation forces introverts to take a step back and avoid the situation altogether. This is also true because many times, introverts tend to think about the worst-case scenario. While intuition is a great thing, it is better to be prepared to avoid any mishaps. If you get embarrassed easily, it is better to avoid situations that can be humiliating. Try not to draw a lot of attention to yourself. But if you want to conquer the fear of humiliation, the best way is to stop caring. This may be quite difficult in the beginning, but with enough time and practice, you will become shameless, which means you will stop caring about what other people think and feel.

Never let other people judge you for being an introverted person. It is a natural thing; that is why you should accept and embrace all your natural, introverted characteristics. You cannot conquer your fears if you cannot face them. When you learn how to conquer and face your fears, you start to grow as a human being. So, try to tackle your fears, even if they seem too nerve-wracking right now. You can tackle all your introversion-related fears, including shyness, small-talk related nervousness, and fear of embarrassment if you spend some time practicing the methods given in this book.

Learn How It Functions

Before countering any strong foe, you need to understand its weaknesses and strengths. You need to have thorough information about it. If fear is interfering in your life, how does it do it? For instance, it can interfere with your professional life, your academic life, and your personal life. You need to understand the physical signs of psychological as well as physical fear. Once you collect all this information, you can start tackling it properly and become more capable of defeating your fear.

Along with the above information, you should also collect raw data from sources such as articles, books, psychology blogs, and mental health professionals.

Be Aware of Your Fear

Once you collect information related to your fear and become familiar with it, you need to start examining how you feel about it. Understand where you feel it in your body. Do you feel it in your throat, chest, or belly? Understand its physicality, so that next time, when you experience it, you will be able to identify it immediately. This way, you will be able to work against it properly. Naming your fear and calling it aloud from time to time will help you tackle it.

Face It

It is crucial to understand and accept your fear. Do not try to deny it or hide it. Introverts often must deal with negative feelings which they try to hide. But hiding these feelings cannot help because hiding does not solve the underlying problem but is only likely to further aggravate the issue. Once you start noticing and not hiding the fear, you can start tackling it by using the various steps given above. It may indeed seem like a difficult task in the beginning, but with patience, dedication, and time you will be able to do it. Don't be too hard on yourself. You need to tackle your fear gradually. If your first attempt does not go as expected, don't worry, just keep pushing. Fear is a sort of habit, and it is difficult to overcome habits. Even the tiniest step will help you progress. With time you will see the new habits taking root. Once these habits settle in, you won't have to make any effort to maintain them in the future.

Remember Why It Matters

Introverts are often surprised when they see extroverts being happy and joyful even in the scariest social scenarios. One of the biggest reasons why extroverts do not appear to be scared is because of how their brains handle social situations. For them, the social situations are pleasurable, and the feeling of pleasure overpowers the feeling of fear.

Introverts are highly concentrated on their feelings, which is why their fear seems to appear bigger than that of extroverts. This is why they tend to avoid social gatherings. But if this is hindering your progress, you need to get over it. Social interactions are crucial while living in society. You need to ask yourself every time before avoiding something whether it is important or not, whether you need to interact with the person or the situation or not, and whether the current conversation will help you in the future or not.

If you do not partake in the current conversation, will it hinder your prospects in the future? Understanding and answering these questions will help you to calm down and think the matter over carefully. It will also help you control and manage your decisions properly. Remember, your conscience is quite selective, so use it carefully. Try to seek a balance between the pros and cons of the situation and then make a solid decision.

Repeat!

Human beings form habits quickly and then stick to the habits for a long time. Our brain forms habits because they help you to manage things more easily. This mechanism is crucial because it allows the brain to save energy for future tasks, as it can use past experiences to reference your response to present challenges. But for this to work properly, you need to concentrate on every situation so that your brain can form patterned responses to past experiences. If your brain forms bad habits, you will suffer in the future. To make your brain strong, you need to put in conscious effort to drive your behavior carefully. You also need to learn how to adjust your behavior so that you can move forward. Remember, perfection is not possible, but this does not mean that you should stop pursuing it.

Fear is a confusing feeling because its main motive is to warn people about impending danger. Our body, when it senses fear, tends to address it with the instinctive flight-or-fight response. Introverts generally choose the first reaction and try to avoid the situation altogether. It is therefore crucial to manage your internalized fear and move forward in the world.

Chapter Ten: Overcoming Social Anxiety and Awkwardness

People often confuse introversion with social anxiety, especially in the case of extroverts who think all introverts are socially awkward. But introversion and social anxiety are distinctly different and mutually exclusive. In this chapter, let us have an in-depth look at social anxiety and introversion.

First, it is necessary to clarify that introversion is not an illness. Introversion is related to how our body uses energy. Social awkwardness and anxiety are related to how you feel in your day-to-day life and how you respond to things you experience. Let's take a look at how to deal with life experiences if you are an introvert who suffers from social anxiety.

Dealing with Social Anxiety as an Introvert

• **Meeting New People**

Meeting new people can be difficult, especially for people who have social anxiety. They become obsessed with small details and are generally nervous about making a good impression. This nervousness is also reflected in the content of the conversation, where socially anxious people tend to ask more questions than answer them. This is a great tactic in the initial stages because everyone likes to talk about themselves, but it becomes old quickly. People who have social anxiety generally find it difficult to initiate a conversation because they tend to overthink things, which sometimes makes them appear tongue-tied.

• **Talking is Fun**

In some respects, socially awkward people are quite similar to introverts. Like introverts, socially awkward people to like to talk if the topic is right up their alley. If the topic is interesting, they can talk a lot about it. Introverts and socially awkward people both tend to think a lot before talking. They prefer to collect themselves and gather information before presenting their point of view. But socially awkward people prefer to listen to other people talk. They can talk to multiple people for a fairly long time, but once their threshold is crossed, they start to melt down.

• **Crowds**

Introverts and socially awkward people will usually try to avoid meeting people in a crowded area. The waiting and small-talk aspect of having dinner in a crowded place can be quite nerve-wracking for people who suffer from social anxiety. They will forget to enjoy the meal and the company, and their focus will be on escaping the situation as soon as possible. So instead of going for a crowded place, socially awkward people should choose a calm and serene place with little to no crowds.

• **Quietness**

Extroverts are often bemused by introverts and socially awkward people being so quiet most of the time. Socially awkward introverts can be insanely quiet; they can maintain their silence even in the most difficult situation, because they enjoy it. They have hobbies that generally involve solitude, such as writing, reading, listening to music, gardening, etc. Being silent helps introverts and socially anxious people to concentrate and contemplate. It provides them a sense of the world that allows them to enjoy the little pleasures of life properly.

- **Books**

Many introverted, socially awkward people are avid readers. These people enjoy the company of books a lot. They tend to talk about books a lot. They always have book recommendations for people. They also like to reread the books that they loved because it gives them a sense of reconnection.

Many times, these people disconnect from the world to enter the reality of the book they are reading. They would rather spend hours on end with their book instead of going to a noisy and crowded party.

- **Sadness**

Due to their inherent tendency to feel emotions intensely, introverts who are socially awkward are often sad. Any simple piece of news can trigger them and can make them sad for a long time. Anxiety is often a gateway to depression. Sometimes introverts try to get out of their sadness by being solitary, but many times this solitude can aggravate the problem. When introverts suffering from social anxiety get triggered, their emotional system collapses.

Thus, introversion and social anxiety may seem mutually exclusive, but a person can have both simultaneously. Being an introvert or a socially anxious person is not a negative thing. It just means that you need to keep an eye on your health and work carefully. Introversion is not a mental illness, but according to many sources, social anxiety is. If you have both, then it is necessary to be bold and be confident. There is nothing wrong with you. You may indeed find certain situations and aspects of your life quite difficult, but it does not mean that you should sit in a corner moping. Be yourself and be yourself confidently! It does not matter if you are an introvert or that you are anxious. Just be bold.

Differences between Social Anxiety and Introversion

In the previous section, we saw how to deal with social anxiety and introversion together. But what are the major differences between these two? In this section, let us have a look at these differences in detail.

- **Introversion is Born; Social Anxiety is *Made***

Introversion is perfectly natural, and it is a part of your personality. You cannot change it, and you cannot cure it because it is not a disease or a disorder. Introversion comes directly from the womb. Socially awkward people are generally introverted but while these two are mutually exclusive, many times introverts tend to be socially awkward because of the lethal combination of genetics and social experiences.

Many things can make a person socially anxious. One of the major reasons why a person can be socially anxious is learning. People tend to learn new things in different new situations, and sometimes the things that they learn are negative. For instance, if your parents are always worried about something, you may learn to worry, cultivating that habit in your mind. This trait then gets enhanced by actions and experiences such as bullying and other such traumatic interactions. People who have social anxiety often tend to think that they are just not up to the mark.

Another aspect of social anxiety is avoidance of interaction. People who have social anxiety tend to avoid things because they do not want to indulge in small talk. They make excuses and even feign illness. In parties, if these people feel nervous, they stare at their phones constantly to avoid interacting with others. Some may even avoid meeting people at parties by hiding in the bathroom.

- **Fear of Being Revealed**

People who have social anxiety tend to believe that there is something inherently wrong with them. This is because they do not believe in themselves, and they believe that they have a lot of flaws that they have kept hidden; most of the time, these supposed flaws are fake and do not exist, yet they convince themselves that they have these flaws.

These flaws can be of a varied nature; they can be physical as well as mental. For instance, they may believe that they turn red when they talk to people, and their palms start to sweat. Some people may feel that the world will laugh at them if they try to voice their opinions. It does not matter what flaws these people think they have; they are scared of them being revealed.

The introverts who do not have social anxiety do not believe that there is something inherently wrong with them. They are not scared about the "big reveal" because they have nothing in particular to hide.

- **Perfectionism and Social Anxiety**

Perfectionism is the bane of human existence. People who strive for perfection apparently do not realize that perfection does not exist. People who have social anxiety try to achieve perfection in social interactions; they try to be as socially flawless as possible. They have an all-or-nothing attitude, which in itself is quite problematic. Socially anxious people are afraid of criticism. They try to be charming and witty to avoid criticism, but it does not always work. When it does not work, it may mentally paralyze the person.

Introverts who do not suffer from social anxiety do not care about these things. They understand that they are not always under the scrutiny of others. They do not anticipate judgment. They tend to follow the natural flow in the conversation. But even if the conversation does not flow naturally and ends up being awkward, they won't think too much about it because ultimately, they do not care that much about how it went.

- **Introversion is Your Way; Social Anxiety *Gets in Your* Way**

Social anxiety is closely related to fear. In fact, social anxiety is almost always channeled through fear. People who have social anxiety tend to avoid gatherings and large crowds because they fear the noise. But some extroverts who are socially anxious can also feel this way. Extroverts love parties, and if social anxiety does not allow them to visit one, they will feel frustrated and angry. If social anxiety is bringing new problems into your life almost every day, then it is recommended you do something about it.

Like socially anxious people, introverts also try to avoid parties; if they end up at a party, they try to leave it as soon as possible. Unlike socially anxious people, they do not care if they leave too early. They do not criticize themselves for leaving early because they know that they just don't find partying interesting enough. They do not judge themselves or feel strange, either. Their choice is not driven by fear; it is only driven by their judgment and mind.

Thus, social anxiety may seem like a kind of introversion in the beginning, but if you delve deep, you will realize that these two things are quite different. But it is possible to overcome social anxiety. You just need to learn how to do it. In the next chapter, we'll have a look at how you can be socially confident even if you are socially awkward.

Chapter Eleven: How to Be Socially Confident

Being socially confident is not a difficult task. With some practice, time, and dedication, anyone can be socially confident. If you tend to avoid social gatherings or sit in a corner when you attend one, don't worry; you are not the only one. There are many people like you in the world, whether introverted or not. Solving this problem is quite easy. You just need to be confident and bold. Let us have a look at how you can become a self-confident and socially adept person in a few simple steps.

Creating a Confident Outlook

• **Accept Yourself**

If you do not accept yourself, no one else is going to accept you either. Introverts love to spend time with themselves, and they hate crowds. This is a natural tendency that you cannot change. You cannot expect to wake up one morning and become an exceptional party animal. If you try to do so, it will only result in undue stress and anxiety. It will lead to the development of more problems instead of solving those you already have. Instead of forcing yourself to be outgoing, try to find a middle ground where you feel comfortable and confident.

Accepting your introverted nature can help you focus on the quality of the conversations you have instead of focusing on the number of conversations you have. Remember, the quantity is not as important as the quality.

- **Confidence is Crucial**

You cannot be socially adept if you are not confident. Becoming confident is not a difficult task; you must talk to people and engage them in such a way that they feel heard. You need to appear bold, but not brash. These things will ultimately enhance your social competence. According to research, social competence is great for your self-confidence and your self-perception. You will start to accept yourself during the various social situations you engage if you know how to do it. Practicing social competence is crucial because it will allow you to create new opportunities for yourself. This happens because when you are socially competent, you will approach more and more new people. This way, you will form new contacts, and you will ultimately find new opportunities as well.

Your self-perception plays an important role in how you act in society. If you do not feel self-confident, you will not act confidently. It is necessary to cut out the negativity from your life if you want to be happy, confident, and sociable, which brings us to our next point.

- **Negativity**

If you want to be a positive and sociable person, you need to *stop being negative.* Negative ideas and thoughts are bad for your social, mental, and physical health. When you are not socially confident, you try to find rationales that confirm your negative thoughts. Whenever you feel that you are too negative, stop right there and try to find the evidence supporting the negative thought. Often, you will find nothing, and thus, you will nip the negative thought in the bud.

For instance, if you think that no one likes you because you are boring, stop and find evidence of how you are not boring and how people like you. This will clear all your doubts, and you will feel free once again.

- **Test Your Beliefs**

Once you begin looking for evidence supporting confidence and positivity, you can try testing them. How people react to something does not depend on you; in fact, you cannot control the reactions of other people. If you believe that you are the reason behind certain reactions, then ignore them. How people react solely depends on them. Avoid making any other assumptions.

For instance, if you see a person making a face, you may feel that he or she is teasing you or is bored with you. Sometimes some people end conversations in mid-flow to get up and go away. Don't worry; instead of blaming yourself, try to see whether there were some other reasons why this happened. If a person makes a face while talking to you, it might be because he or she is not comfortable in his or her seat or is not feeling well. If a person ends a conversation abruptly, he or she may have a task that needs to be handled immediately. Or he or she may be an introvert and require some "me" time as soon as possible.

- **Compassion**

If you show compassion toward others, you will receive compassion in return. An exchange of compassion creates a healthy atmosphere conducive to conversation. It can lead to positive interactions that can help to make you more self-confident. It will allow you to understand how to pick up on social cues. It will also help you become more empathetic.

- **Expectations**

When we interact with people, we tend to have expectations regarding some sort of response from them. If you tend to expect a lot from the people or the interaction, you will often end up feeling dissatisfied. This is because you did not have healthy expectations of the interaction. Never take responsibility for how people act around you; that is their decision.

If you are trying to talk to a person and he or she does not respond positively, do not beat yourself up for it. Just shake it off and move on. If a person does not want to talk to you, it is not your problem. It is his or her problem. You cannot be friends with everyone, and not everyone will want to be friends with you. This is perfectly normal.

• Show Interest in Others

A conversation takes place between two or more people. If you only talk about yourself throughout the conversation, no one will be interested in talking to you. You should be able to make your conversation partner comfortable. He or she should feel that you hear and value him or her. This characteristic is known as social competency, and it is an important step in being socially confident. You should try to understand the verbal as well as non-verbal signals and use them to make others feel comfortable. This will help you hone your social skills.

For instance, crossing the arms and avoiding eye contact are two gestures that make people seem uninviting. So, if you want to appear inviting and engaging, avoid using these gestures.

• **Nonverbal Communication**

Introverts do not like to talk, but you can *talk nonverbally* with the help of your body language. Try to adopt a body language that makes you seem more confident. Use body language poses, also known as "power poses", to help you look confident and bold.

There are many different power poses, and a lot of information is available about them online. Adopt a few of them and see the difference for yourself.

Examples:

• Sitting up tall and keeping your chest expanded.

• Placing your hands on the table while sitting on a chair.

• Standing with your shoulders and arms wide open.

• Smiling quite often.

• Making eye contact while talking to people.

- Not fidgeting.
- Clarity of speech.

Along with the gestures and behaviors mentioned above, you can find many more online.

If you can voice your opinions clearly and lucidly, it will make you appear bold and confident. You need to learn how to speak with confidence. Your partner or audience should be able to hear you clearly and understand you properly. Adjust the pitch of your voice. You need to learn how to communicate properly because skillful verbal communication can help you appear comfortable in social gatherings and help people to understand you better.

Mumbling is a sign of low confidence; it also portrays disinterest. It will make people think that you are not comfortable in a conversation.

- **Pace**

Mere clarity of voice cannot help you to be a great speaker; you also need to control and modulate your pace. Your pace should not be too slow or too fast. People should be able to understand you properly. Sometimes, people tend to speak too fast when they are nervous. Speaking too fast will make things difficult for other people, as they will not be able to understand you. To make sure that you are speaking at a normal pace, take steady breaths at regular intervals while speaking. This way, you will be able to control your pace.

If you see that you are speaking too fast, pause for a moment and start speaking slowly once again.

- **Listening Skills**

You can't be a great speaker if you are not a great listener. You need to learn how to listen to people in order to learn how to talk to them. Try to focus on what people are saying. Think about it. This way, you will be able to formulate concrete answers to their questions. You will be able to respond to them appropriately. Your answers need to be thoughtful and calming. If you listen to people while talking, it indicates that you are indeed interested in what they want to say. This will show that you not only care about their ideas and opinions but respect their person as well.

When you are nervous, you tend to pay a lot of attention to yourself. This is natural, but it is still liable to make other people feel uncomfortable. They should not feel that you are not interested in what they are saying.

Do not interrupt people. Instead, let the person finish his or her thought and *then* make your argument.

- **Social Situations**

In the last few tips, we saw how you could become socially confident, but you can't truly be confident until you use these tips in real life. To practice your social confidence skills, you need to put yourself in social settings from time to time. These social situations can help you become more confident and will allow you to practice properly. With time and practice, your social skills will develop, and you will become more and more confident. If you frequently engage yourself in social situations, it will help you become more comfortable in them, and it will reduce your anxiety as well. Instead of putting yourself in only certain kinds of social situations, try to find a variety of social occasions.

Try to initiate conversations. Initiating a conversation is not difficult. You can start with a simple hello, or you can pay a person a compliment and then take the conversation further.

- **Roleplay**

Role-playing really revamps your life if done correctly. Whenever you want to practice your social skills, just ask a friend or a trusted family member to help you. Ask him or her to pretend to be a stranger. Then you can practice your skills with him or her. These practice sessions will help you form an informal script in your head that you can use when you meet real strangers. Just create a simple and flexible format so that you will be able to use it with a lot of people.

- Friends

If you find initiating a conversation difficult, don't worry. Just ask a friend to introduce you to people. Meeting friends of your friends is a good way to increase your social circle. You can also practice your communication skills without having to introduce yourself to new people. Ask your friend to introduce you and then take part in the conversation as it naturally unfolds.

- Socialize in New Settings

As we discussed, you need to put yourself in a variety of social settings. Once you get used to a place, you will become comfortable with it. But if you want to enhance your new-found confidence, you need to visit places where no one knows you. This will challenge your self-confidence. If you do not want to be at a crowded party, find a small gathering in which to meet new people. It is recommended that you always be on the lookout for a place to find new and interesting people. This will enhance your confidence immensely.

Small gatherings can be of any sort. For instance, you can find and meet people at a gym, in a book club or hobby club, etc. These places will offer you lots of opportunities to start conversations.

Chapter Twelve: How to Become More Sociable as an Introvert

Introverted people are often considered mysterious, but generally, men face the brunt of being introverted more than women. Men are supposed to display their strength and prowess; they are supposed to take the initiative most of the time. These aspects are crucial for them because they directly affect their personal and professional success. If you are introverted and want to become more sociable for personal or professional reasons, this section will help you do so. It contains various tried and tested tips and methods that will help you become a socially adept introvert in no time. You just need to practice them regularly to make yourself more confident and bolder.

Talking

Many people believe that you need to talk a lot to be sociable. Introverts tend to avoid this, because introverts do not particularly like talking. But don't worry, no one expects you to talk a lot. You just need to calm down and follow the flow of the conversation. When you do need to say something, just say it in a relaxed tone.

Embrace Your Introverted Side

Many people try to change their introverted characteristics because they feel that being introverted is wrong. But this is a myth. Introversion is perfectly natural and normal. Introversion with confidence provides you with a mysterious aura that is irresistible to both genders. You need to learn how to be comfortable in your skin and be confident. Your self-confidence will help you tackle all the awkwardness that is associated with introversion.

Conversation Starters

Nowadays, due to professional and personal commitments, people are likely to meet new people almost every day. This can be nerve-wracking for introverts because they do not like to make small talk. If you are ever stuck in a similar situation, don't worry. Just plan things out beforehand. Instead of meeting a stranger at a random place, choose your places carefully. Your choice should allow you ample conversation topics, so that whenever you sense an awkward silence coming over the conversation, just pick a topic and talk about it. Meeting at a restaurant is a far better option than meeting in a park.

Listen, Think, and Respond

Listening is a great skill that is generally associated with introversion. Introverts love to listen and then think things over. But they rarely respond quickly. If you do not want to scare away your partner, it is recommended to not only listen and think but respond. This will keep the conversation moving forward.

Emphasize Your Strengths

Introverts are born with various skills that are generally known as the characteristics of introversion. Some of these skills include listening, honesty, and great observation skills. If you have some of these skills, be bold about them, and do not hide them. Let them shine brightly. They will surely help you get noticed and ultimately be more sociable.

Practice

Sociable people tend to know what to say, when to say it, and how to say it. Some extroverts are born with this skill, but others learn it with practice. You can learn it, too, by talking to strangers and finding interesting conversation topics. With practice, you, too, will become socially adept.

Entertainer

A great way to become socially accepted is to entertain people. Some people can entertain others without looking silly. If you are not one of these people, then avoid trying to be an entertainer. Introverts rarely feel comfortable being the center of attention. So, instead of forcing yourself into the limelight, stay back and enjoy things from a distance.

Style

Your clothes and style can help you express things that you cannot express verbally. If you find it difficult to talk and express yourself properly through words, let your clothes and accessories speak for you. Upgrading your style is especially recommended if you do not feel confident in your clothes. While being confident in one's skin is necessary, you can expedite the process by being confident in your clothes as well.

Friendliness

Instead of thinking of people as strangers, think of them as friends you only just met. If you treat strangers like friends, you will not feel as awkward. Just use the conversation tactics that you use with your regular friends. This way, you will not be nervous, and you will be able to hold a conversation successfully.

Alone Time

Remember that introversion is normal, and you cannot let go of it. It is your personality, and you need to tap into your introverted side from time to time. You still need to recharge yourself by enjoying some "me" time alone. This time is essential because it will allow you to have fresh ideas.

In summary: to become more sociable, an introvert just needs to become more self-confident. Having self-confidence will automatically boost your social skills. Do not worry a lot about the impressions that you may make on people; just show up, be yourself, and relax.

Chapter Thirteen: How to Network and Make Friends as an Introvert

Finding Someone Who Understands You

Finding people who understand you is difficult. It becomes even more difficult when you are an introvert who loves solitude. Contrary to popular belief, introverts need friends, too. While it is easy to make friends when you are young or are in school, it becomes quite difficult to meet new people and become friends with them when you are an adult. There are many reasons for this; the lack of meeting space, lack of topics of conversation, and lack of time and energy are some reasons why adults find it difficult to make new friends. For introverts, it is even more difficult because they find meeting strangers exhausting.

Introverts tend to be choosy. They cannot be friends with just any random person. They tend to be selective and only try to be friends with people whom they can trust and understand. This is because introverts do not have a lot of social energy, and they do not want to waste it on random people. Extroverts are like large party halls where one can accommodate and entertain a lot of people simultaneously, while introverts are like luxury suites, which means they let only exclusive people enter.

Some people believe that an extrovert can't be close friends with an introvert and vice versa, but this is false. If your friend understands you properly and clicks with you, you will surely appreciate him or her. In this section, let us have a look at some tips that can help you find friends that understand you.

- **Think About Your Acquaintances**

Instead of trying to find new people to be friends with, you can connect with your acquaintances and become friends with them. Everyone has a lot of acquaintances in their life; just check out the ones you find interesting and initiate contact with them. You will make a new friend in no time!

- First Moves

Almost all introverts hate initiating contact. If you are one of these, then you will wait for someone else to talk to you first. This is because you are afraid of rejection. You do not want to get rejected and feel embarrassed or humiliated. This can bring out your self-doubt issues, which in turn can be quite harmful to your mental health. If you have faced a lot of rejection in your life before this, you may not initiate contact with anyone in the future. You feel discouraged and sad. But this discouragement can wreak havoc in your life.

Passivity, especially in adulthood, is problematic. If you act passively in making new contacts, you will find it hard to make new friends in your life. People will never flock to you trying to be your friend; you need to make some effort to contact them. Friendship is a mutual relationship; both parties need to make an equal effort to make it successful. No one will try to become your friend if you do not make any effort. Take matters into your own hands and initiate conversations. Take the first step instead of waiting for others to do so.

- **Masks**

When you meet new people, it is only natural to try to make them feel comfortable. This is especially true for introverted people who want others to like them. But this is a difficult task because you need to maintain an aura of happiness all the time to do so. It takes a lot of work to do this, and ultimately it will not produce any significant results.

You cannot be friends with someone if you are not "real," and to appeal to someone, people tend to hide their quirks and negative aspects, putting forward only their positive side. They literally create a façade, and everyone knows that keeping up a façade for a long time is not only difficult but impossible. You will soon start to hate your friends because the facade will make you miserable. It will suck up your energy and will leave you feeling tired and empty.

So, instead of creating a façade just so that people can like you, try to present your true self. Be confident about yourself and don't worry if people don't appreciate you in the beginning. Your vulnerability will allow you to connect with other people effectively.

- **Ask Questions**

Two things are almost givens in this world: people love talking about themselves, and introverts like listening and contemplating. You can use these two factors to your advantage. Whenever you meet new people, talk a few minutes about yourself and then ask questions about them. They will surely appreciate your interest in them, and you will be able to conduct a successful conversation. Use your listening skills to cover your weak verbal skills.

- **Notice How You Feel**

This is a great way to test whether you enjoy hanging out with your new friend or not. When you hang out with the friend, do you feel incredibly tired, or do you feel happy, and perhaps energized? As an introvert, it is perfectly natural to feel kind of tired after spending time with a new person, but this tiredness is often pleasing. If you feel excessively tired and uncomfortable, then perhaps the new friendship is not meant to be.

Emotionally needy people generally seek introverts to display their emotional baggage. As introverts are good listeners, emotionally needy people tend to use them as sounding boards, or, sometimes, a metaphorical punching bag. Introverts, who prefer others to initiate contact, are generally happy in this relationship in the beginning, but with time, they realize that they are not really friends with the person. If you are ever caught in a similar situation, it is recommended you back away gradually and break ties with him or her gently. You do not want relationships that drain you.

- **Awkwardness**

Many introverts tend to stay away from people because they feel awkward around others. Even when they meet new people, they keep their positive characteristics, such as a fun personality or quirkiness, hidden. Their true selves only come out when they feel comfortable with the person. But this way you may miss the chance to meet new people.

Don't worry if you feel awkward with a person in the beginning: in time you will become more comfortable and will start enjoying your friend's company.

- **Meetups**

You cannot be friends with a person if you do not hang out with each other from time to time; ask your friend to meet you and hang out with you at least once a week. A simple lunch on the weekends will suffice. You can also go for a group hangout so that you will be able to meet new people. It is recommended to schedule hangout sessions; in this way, you will be able to form a routine. *Introverts love routines.*

- **Go Slowly**

Friendships do not happen overnight, especially in the case of adults. It takes time for a relationship to mature and develop properly. Do not try to force a friendship. Let it develop gradually; a gradually developed friendship will always be better than a simple, overnight relationship.

Remember, the quality of friends is more important than the number of friends. It is better to have a small circle of extremely close and trustworthy friends than to have a lot of shallow acquaintances.

Making Friends in the Modern World

Introverted people find it quite difficult to make new friends, especially when they are forced to do so. It can be quite an exhausting experience. In the last section, we saw how an introvert could make new friends. Many other ways can help you to become friends with people. Modern amenities can make it easier to make new friends. Finding friends on the Internet has become quite easy but becoming friends in real life with your online friends can be quite difficult. In this section, let us have a look at how you can use online methods to make online friends and turn them into friends in real life as well.

• Blog Posts

Blogs are a great way to express yourself and present your ideas to the world. A lot of people read blogs frequently, though only a few people comment on them. Blogs are not meant to be a form of a one-way conversation. You can contact the blog writer and show your appreciation of him or her by commenting on positive things about their blog. You can also use this method to find and make new friends. Just by reading the blogs and commenting on them, you can form positive relationships. You can then continue those friendships in the form of emails and social media.

Some people tend to use blogs as a sounding board where they just put their ideas. They do not want any comments or replies to their content. But most blog writers appreciate it when people comment on their blogs and compliment their hard work. If you frequently comment on particular blogs, you will ultimately form a strong bond with the writer.

• Join Facebook Groups

Facebook groups have become a great way to meet people who think alike and like the same things. Finding new friends is quite easy on social media. It is easy to become friends with likeminded people. Join some groups related to things you are interested in. For instance, a reading group, a cooking group, or a movie group can help you make friends with ease. Just post your experiences in the group and comment on the experiences of others. Show that you are genuinely interested in talking to people and interacting with them.

Many people have found lifelong friends with the help of Facebook and other social media sites and apps. There are many groups on Facebook that are especially great for introverts. Just search for them on the site and enjoy making new friends.

- **Tweet People**

Another great way to meet new people and talk to them online is Twitter. Twitter may be quite daunting, especially in the beginning, because it moves quickly, and there is a text limit. The concept of DMs can be quite confusing. Still, Twitter is a great way to connect with people if you are an introvert.

Twitter is especially great for an introvert because it allows you to listen without having to talk to people. As made sufficiently clear before, introverts love listening. Twitter can allow you to listen to people by "following" them. You can stay up to date with people without having to talk to them all the time. You can also physically meet the people that you met on Twitter. This way, you will be able to find some "real" friends easily.

- **Twitter Chats**

Once you understand how "following" and "lists" work on Twitter, you can begin to use other options. For instance, Twitter can be used to have some meaningful interactions and can also help you to build great relationships. To do this, you can use the Twitter chat option to meet new people and talk to them.

Twitter chats are comparatively more regular than meeting people in bars. You can meet the same person over and over and form a great relationship with him or her. If you find it difficult to handle Twitter chat on your mobile device, drop it and just use your computer. The interface is much better on the computer than on mobile devices.

- **Setup Skype Dates**

Video conferencing platforms such as Google Hangouts, Skype, and Zoom are great services with which to meet and talk to new people. These services can allow you to be in your comfort zone and meet new people without any problem. You can sit in your home office or your bedroom and talk to people from all over the world. You can literally be sitting in one corner of the U.S. and talking to a person sitting in Indonesia.

Skype and videoconferences are great ways to contact people. You can also have a one-on-one chat with friends from another part of the world.

- **Hire Them**

Another way to meet new people and become friends with them is by hiring them. If you have a small business, you can hire new employees and become friends with them. This option is not always feasible, as people do not work for free. So, whenever you need a new employee, you will, of course, have to spend some amount of money for their services. But if you can hire some people, then it will be a great experience as you will be able to form a strong bond with them.

If you do not have a business of your own, you can become friends with your colleagues at work. Gone are the days when people used to think that it was a bad decision to be friends with your colleagues. Get out and become friends with them!

- **Ask for Intros**

This is another great way to make new friends. If you want to be friends with someone, but you do not know them, then you can ask a mutual friend to introduce you. People love helping other people because it makes them feel important. If you ask someone politely to introduce you to someone else, he or she will be glad to do so.

You can do this frequently to make new friends. Even if you do not end up being friends with the person, you can still add him or her as a contact. It will certainly pay off in the long term. Asking someone to introduce you to someone else will allow you to form a close bond with the first person as well. This method can yield doubled results.

- **Attend Conferences**

If you are finished meeting people online and now want to meet people physically, there are many new methods to do so. Gone are the days when you could only meet people in bars and clubs. Now you can meet and make friends with people anywhere. Every month, there are many different conferences and conventions happening. Just find some conventions that you find interesting and attend them. Here you will be able to find new people and talk to them. This is a great way to make new friends and perhaps get in touch with your old friends as well, finding them there because you have mutual interests.

- **Introduce Others**

If you cannot find someone to introduce you to a person, you can introduce other people to other individuals. So, if you feel that two people should know each other because they will enjoy being friends, just introduce them. You will act as a sort of friendship matchmaker. This way, you will be able to connect with a lot of people and will be able to form strong bonds with them. When you connect with other people, they connect with you as well. Thus, you end up making new friends from all directions.

So, instead of making excuses, get up and get out of your house (or not) and try to make new friends. If you do not make an effort, you will not be able to make new friends. Use the modern amenities mentioned in this book to help you tackle the world of adult friendship. Don't worry; with ample time and patience, you will be able to forge strong lifelong bonds without any problem.

Chapter Fourteen: Introverts in Professional Settings

Introverts who work in offices tend to be surrounded by colleagues and employees throughout the day. People tend to exchange stories, make acquaintances, make friends, form contacts, etc. It is recommended that you join the conversation and become friends with other people. These contacts are crucial if you want to climb the ladder of success. But most introverts cannot do this, as they are afraid to approach strangers and talk to them.

Around one third or more of the people you meet are introverts. These people prefer intimate settings and events as opposed to the larger gathering enjoyed by extroverts. They do not like excessively stimulating and loud atmospheres. But generally, society is more involved with and aligned toward extroverts. This is especially true in the professional world where introverts are treated as second-rate citizens.

But it does not matter. You need to strive and work hard if you want to succeed in the corporate world, especially if you are an introvert. You need to work hard at getting to know your colleagues. In this section, let's consider some tips that can help you become successful in a professional setting.

Be Yourself

While this may sound like a cliché, it is still true. You cannot succeed if you are not true to yourself. Beating yourself up every day just because you are not an extrovert will not take you anywhere; rather, it leads to the development of more and more problems. While it is true that having certain extroverted characteristics can help you immensely in the world, expecting yourself to behave and act just like extroverts is illogical and childish. Instead of doing this, try to make your introverted personality stand out.

If you do not feel comfortable in crowds and prefer small groups, then don't beat yourself up about it. There is nothing wrong with feeling more comfortable in a small group. You need to understand your characteristics and use them as your assets. For instance, introverts are blessed with great thinking and listening skills. You can use these to form good, intimate, long-lasting relationships with people. Just focus on things that matter and ignore the ones that do not.

Redefine Your Approach

Try to redefine your approach toward life and your career. If you avoid meeting people because you hate crowds, try to meet them in more intimate settings. Arrange your meetings in smaller offices or cafes. You can also conduct meetings at golf courses or tennis courts. Just find a place that you find intimate and comfortable. This way, you will be able to talk to your partner without any inhibitions.

Focus on Remarkability

According to many studies, our brains are well suited to respond to new and interesting situations. This means that if the situation is new, you can make exciting memories. So, if you want to meet new people but are scared or nervous about it, make the meeting exciting by incorporating something new into it. For instance, if you own a farm, conduct the meeting *on the farm*. Try some new activities to make things exciting and memorable.

Take Baby Steps

If approaching people and initiating conversations scare you, don't worry. Just take baby steps and move on slowly. Always try to step out of your complacent zone slowly, one step at a time.

Start with a safety net. Start the conversation and move on slowly. If you find the experience intimidating, don't worry; keep on practicing, and move forward.

Take Advantage of The Winner Effect

The "winner effect" means that whenever a person wins, their body receives a pleasant shock from the brain. This pleasant shock is great because it quickly boosts your confidence for a while. The more you win, the better your confidence levels will be. So, whenever you plan to meet new people, try to win at something.

Tell Yourself the Right Things

Recontextualize things. When you are scared about things, try to think about them from a positive point of view. This can help you enhance your performance. For instance, if you hate speaking and generally get nervous about meetings, do not talk a lot; instead, listen and make some interesting and skillful comments. This way, you will be able to participate in the conversation without feeling flustered. You won't have to do small talk either!

Ask for a Warm Introduction

If you want to make a connection at a social event but are scared to do so, don't worry. Just ask a friend to introduce you to someone. Initiating a conversation can be difficult, which is why many introverts fail to make the effort. Instead of making the necessary effort, introverts tend to sit back in a corner and not talk to people at all. Instead of doing this, explain the situation to a friend and ask him or her to introduce you. This way, you will be able to talk to the person and make a new contact without facing any severe emotional discomfort.

If All Else Fails, Outsource

If you have tried all the options above but have still failed, don't worry; there are other options that you can try. A simple way to connect with people is by asking people to introduce you to others. Ask a friend or a colleague to be a matchmaker for you. This way, you can connect to the person and your friend as well.

It does not matter whether you are an extrovert or an introvert. Anyone can find good, close, and life-long friends, guides, mentors, and influencers through others, but it takes effort. Try these tips to find out which ones suit you the most; they will surely help you become more comfortable around people, and you will be making new friends in no time.

Chapter Fifteen: Tips for Maintaining Relationships

Relationships are exciting, but they can be difficult. They are especially scary for introverts who do not know how to initiate contact. Introverts feel multiple emotions when they try to initiate romantic contacts. While extroverts only feel the giddiness and butterflies-in-the-stomach feeling associated with love, introverts may feel nervousness, fear, and anxiety. The thought of getting into a relationship is enthralling, but it can also be embarrassing, scary, and strange for introverts.

Most introverts want to have a strong and close romantic relationship, but they are generally uncertain about how to go about it. Some introverts believe that dating can only work for them if they can find their soulmate. Due to this hunt for the perfect soulmate, they tend to miss out on many good opportunities to meet excellent people. Introverts can surely find some great people if they start to come out of their shells and make some effort.

In this section, let us have a look at some common tips that can help you achieve a great relationship.

Remove Your Inhibitions

If you like someone and want to go out with them, do not confuse yourself with a gaggle of questions. Just be bold and simply *ask them out immediately.* Generally, when you are an introvert, you tend to think a lot about your prospective date. You are scared about it because you do not know whether it will work out or not. If you do think that it will work, you tend to concentrate on how it will become the best relationship in your life. This amount of fantasizing will only lead to the development of major problems. Introverts love to analyze the past and dream about the future, but many times this makes them ignore the present. Avoid doing this.

Go One Step at a Time

Introverts tend to think a lot before taking serious steps, and in the case of relationships, this may slow the process because of their tendency to daydream. Introverts tend to dream a lot about the future of their relationship. While some amount of fantasizing is okay, try to keep it limited. Instead of dreaming of spending your whole lives together, try to get to know your date better. Understand his or her likes, hobbies, dislikes, goals, work, family, education, friends, etc. Check whether your wavelengths match with each other or not. Avoid jumping to positive or negative conclusions. Reflect on your feelings and think about them carefully. Use your introvert's powers of thinking.

Build the Rapport

It is crucial to build a good rapport with the person you are trying to date. Instead of focusing on yourself, try to focus on your date. Understand their feelings, emotions, and thoughts. While thinking about the date, try to find out your date's ideas about you. Introverts generally tend to *detach from* and *attach to* people too soon. Try to maintain a balance, or your relationship will suffer.

Tell Them What You Are Like

Introverts can be confusing to many people. If your date does not understand you, he or she may think that you are moody and dull. In such a case, it is better to be honest, and tell your date how and what you feel. Let them know how solitude is crucial for you and how you need the vigor you get from isolation. Your date should know the future of your relationship. If your date understands your needs, then great! If not, it is better to move on right away.

Talk about Things That Are Important to You

Introverts and extroverts consider things differently. For instance, the perceptions and values that introverts hold are different from the perceptions and values that extroverts possess. If you are an introvert who is dating an extrovert, sit down and discuss what things are important for both of you individually and as a couple. Sharing and being honest in a relationship is essential.

It does not have to be extremely personal. You can share simple needs such as how you like small crowds and quiet places. This way, your partner will understand your needs properly.

Demonstrate Your Strengths

If you are operating under the notion that introverts are disliked all over the world, then drop it immediately! This is a false notion that has been perpetuated by inconsiderate stereotypes. People love introverts as much as they do extroverts. Instead of hiding your characteristics, display them. Wear them on your sleeve with pride. Use your characteristics and make them your strengths. This way, you will be true to yourself and will be able to make your relationship successful.

Chapter Sixteen: Tips on Developing Strong Relationships

In the previous chapter, we covered how difficult it is for introverts to get into relationships and maintain them; because the world is largely focused on extroverts and their needs and desires, introverts generally do not get enough attention. They are not talked about a lot, either. This is typical of all walks of life, be it professional or personal.

If you find it difficult to get into or maintain a relationship because you are an introvert, don't worry. Use these tricks along with the tips mentioned in the previous chapter to come out of your shell. These tips will surely help you to develop a good relationship.

- **Meaningful Conversations**

Liking your partner for superficial reasons will lead to catastrophic results. This is because a relationship cannot survive just based on superficial likes and dislikes. If you want a relationship to work, you need to understand the theories and possibilities of it. You should be able to form a deep and close bond with the person. Introverts love to think and talk about ideas. They prefer to talk a lot about things that they love. They do not care for single-word answers if the topic is interesting. While the term has received much flak over the past few years, it is true; introverts are "sapiosexual". They love people who are cultured and intelligent. They like to be with people who are timeless, aware, and classy.

They would rather be with people who are good conversationalists than those who are into superficial things alone. They do not like smooth talkers, and they would rather have someone challenge them intellectually. Introverts love it when people ask them thought-provoking questions.

• **Less Stimulating Environments**

The brains of introverts get stimulated easily. This means that they do not need a lot of stimulating situations to become happy and achieve pleasure. Introverts do not need to go to exciting parties or large gatherings to feel happy. They hate places where they need to shout just to get their ideas heard in public.

If you are an introvert who finds dating difficult, sit down and try to find the reasons behind it. Many times, introverts avoid dating because dating entails going out of the house and meeting people in noisy and crowded places such as bars and clubs. These places can be overwhelming for you. They will also exhaust you quickly, and you will end up feeling sad and desolate.

If you want to enjoy your date, visit a far less crowded area. As a person who gets overwhelmed easily, it can be quite daunting to visit a heavily crowded event or places such as a theme park or a concert. Instead of going to places like this, try to visit other, quieter, and more serene places. For instance, instead of picking a club as your date venue, go to a small café. Instead of visiting that popular buffet place, why not go to a small, relatively unknown restaurant where the food is delicious, and the ambiance is peaceful? The venues of your dates are quite important because they allow you to study your potential partner. They allow you to understand his or her personality, and they make you feel comfortable and relaxed. A person who is relaxed and comfortable thinks more clearly than a person who is anxious and scared.

- **Slow and Steady**

Introverts like to take things slowly. You would rather go on multiple dates before choosing a partner. You prefer to collect information about your date and understand their motives, life goals, and personality. You rarely display affection toward someone if you do not understand them and know them thoroughly. It may make you seem strange in the beginning, but that does not matter; with ample self-control and patience, you can enjoy a date properly. Remember, a relationship cannot survive if it is only based on superficial things; you must see what lies at the core of the relationship, *and your date.* Inform your date that you prefer to take things slowly, and then watch their reaction. If they seem to be okay with it, great! If not, adjust your priorities slightly.

- **Sensitivity**

Introverts are sensitive, and they like sensitive people. If your partner is not sensitive to your needs and desires, then your relationship will not survive. Don't bottle up your emotions, because they will eventually explode! You need to find a person who is equally sensitive to you. This does not mean that you should look only for an introvert, as many extroverts can be quite sensitive as well. While introverts do not mind conflict, they would rather stay away from it. If you and your date fight a lot, sit down and contemplate that.

- **Get Out of Your Head**

Introverts tend to overthink and overanalyze a lot. It is difficult for them to be in the moment, especially when their mind jumps from one point to the next. It is a natural phenomenon and is a part of being an introvert. If your date finds it silly, let them know why you are this way; he or she will understand. Most of the time, when you are not in the moment, you are perhaps thinking of what to say next or what should be your next move. This is important because it allows you to control the future of your relationship. You don't want it to fail. By looking at the relationship from various points of view, you can prevent that from happening.

• **Read Between the Lines**

Introverts like to read between the lines because it reveals things that the conversation does not. Introverts are born with great thinking and observation skills and are highly focused on things that they like. They are subtle and not brash. Use your powers to understand your date, noticing the nuances of the conversation. Notice the body language and gestures, pay close attention to what your date says and the way they say it. Even the smallest cues can help you understand whether there is some future to this relationship or not. If you ever feel that nothing can be done about this relationship or if you see some red flags, move on and find someone better. If you find a person problematic in the first meeting, you are bound to find them problematic in all your future meetings. So instead of giving people the benefit of the doubt, just move on.

• **Need for Space**

Introverts need a lot of space and time to think things over. You need solitude to think about matters. This solitude is essential because it allows you to recharge your energy. Without energy, you cannot date people properly as you cannot skillfully answer or ask questions. Your date must understand that you need your solitude from time to time. If you find your date to be too suffocating or overbearing, it is better to break things off immediately. A suffocating relationship will make you suffer, and it will make you hide deep within your shell. If you ever feel that your data is being overbearing, let them know. If they try to change their behavior, all is good, but if they don't, then move on.

• **Quality Time**

No matter how many hours you spend together, if you do not find it interesting, you will probably never go on another date with him/her. For introverts, quality matters more than quantity. If you like a person and you go on a date with him or her, only to realize that they have nothing good to say, move on. You will not be able to spend quality time with this person, and you will surely suffer in the long term. You need to gain something from a conversation, as mindless small talk will take you nowhere. If your date cannot keep you interested, even for a few minutes, there is no future to this relationship anyway. It is better to move on now than to create a scene later.

- ## Be Yourself

We live in a world that is obsessed with self-improvement. Everyone is trying to improve all the time and work toward their own betterment. While it is commendable to work on self-improvement, it is necessary to check what things come under the umbrella term of "self-improvement." For instance, introverts are often forced to adopt the characteristics of extroverts because people believe that these characteristics are better than the ones that introverts have. Since their childhood, introverts are forced to be conditioned and molded in such a way that they end up being a faux extrovert. As mentioned already, this is impossible; introverts cannot become extroverts or vice versa. This dehumanizing process should be stopped immediately. If you, as a child, went through such trauma, it is possible that you may still be suffering from it. It is okay, but do not take your baggage everywhere you go; try to adjust your orientation and tackle it as a problem instead.

Instead of trying to appease your date by showing how extroverted you are, accept your true self and be who you are. Do not hide your true colors. Be bold and beautiful and let the flag of introversion fly.

- ## Don't Assume Anything

Do not assume anything when you date someone. Use your introvert's instincts; sit down and relax, thinking and mulling over your ideas. Silence can be quite confusing to extroverts, so let them know that you like silence and that it does not mean anything negative. You should allow your date to understand that you are an introvert and that you look at the world from a different point of view. Do not presume that your date will be ready to adjust to you. Many extroverts and, in fact, many introverts, do not know how to deal with introverts. That is perfectly okay, because the world is centered on extroverts. So, instead of forcing your date to try to understand you, or falsely assuming that they understand you already, try to let them know the nature of your personality. This is not a form of warning. Rather, it is being bold and confident about your true self. Remember, no one will accept you if you do not accept yourself.

Chapter Seventeen: How to Optimize Your Introvert Superpower

Every person with every personality type is born with particular traits and characteristics that can either hinder their progress or help it. Introverts have various characteristics that are often looked down upon in today's world. But instead of ignoring these characteristics, you can use them and modify them in such a way that they can help you in achieving your goals. In this chapter, let us have a look at how your introverted characteristics can help you in your day-to-day life.

Introverts and Career Options

Finding a good career option is often difficult for introverts because of the various characteristics and traits they possess. Introversion is not a single concept; rather, it is a compilation of various personality and emotional traits that are present or absent in people to varying degrees. This makes the task of understanding introverts quite complex. Introversion can be divided into various categories, but the most common categories that we have already discussed are social, thinking, anxious, or inhibited. To choose a career, first, find out what kind of introvert you are.

In this section, you will find a long list of various career options that are suitable for introverts. For the convenience of the reader, these career options are divided according to the types of introversion mentioned above. Do remember that these types tend to overlap a lot, and no one can say for sure that they belong to only one of the above types. So, you should select career options according to your personality style.

Gone are the days when people used to believe that introverts were only good for certain low-paying jobs. Now people know that introverts can prove to be an asset if you know how to use them. The variety of career options given in this section proves the fact that introverts have a lot of career options in which they can perform well with ease.

Remember that this section is meant for reading only. It is always recommended to contact a career counselor before picking any of the following careers as your permanent job. This way, you will be able to understand whether you are really meant for the job or not.

Social Introvert Jobs

Social introversion sounds quite paradoxical because introverts are well known for avoiding social settings. While it may sound dubious or conflicting, this term refers to introverts who do not like getting into social situations and who like to live and think in solitude. It is a well-known fact that introverts love solitude because solitude allows them to recharge and refresh. If they cannot find "alone time", they would rather be with a small group of people instead of being stuck with a large crowd.

It should be noted that the introverts who fall into this category face little or no social anxiety; they merely lean toward finding smaller social gatherings where they won't have to interact with a lot of people.

Social introverts are known to be quite loyal. They understand their own boundaries as well as others'. They would rather develop strong relationships with people instead of attacking or ignoring them. Introverts rarely accept new friends in their social circle. But if the person becomes a part of the inner circle, he or she will never feel alone again; introverts love to take care of their friends.

Social introverts are quite complex, which is why there are a lot of work options available.

If you are a social introvert, pay close attention to the nature of your potential future work environments. A lot of people who are social introverts tend to prefer working from home or similar spaces. Most social introverts try to avoid workplaces that are too noisy, crowded, or full. They would never choose to work in a place that does not offer them privacy. But your career does not depend upon these factors a lot. You can enjoy most of these factors in a lot of different careers if your employer understands your needs.

But there exist many careers in which you do not need to interact with a lot of people anyway. Many of these careers include various trades and skill-based occupations. Let us have a look at some good career options for social introverts.

- **Database Administrator**

These people are responsible for handling data in big firms, industries, and offices. It is a good-paying job.

- **Private Chef**

The nature of this job depends on where you decide to work. For instance, if you are a private chef to a billionaire, you will be paid well to make exotic food for a single individual or family, with only an occasional party of varying size.

- **Electrical or Electronic Engineering Technician**

You do not have to talk to a lot of people in this job, and spend a lot of time exercising your penchant for precise thinking and problem solving.

- **Mechanical Drafter**

This is a great option for people who are artistically inclined and detail oriented.

- **Civil or architectural drafter**

This is great for people who are good at management and planning. It is also a satisfying option for introverts who are into culture and art.

- **Plumber**

Plumbing does not involve a lot of talking to strangers. It is a great job option for people who like to fix things.

- **Commercial driver**

While drivers, especially commercial drivers, must face a lot of strangers every day, it does not matter because you do not have to interact with them.

- **Industrial machinery mechanic**

Industrial machinery mechanics do not need to interact with a lot of people, and they can often choose their work hours.

- **Heavy equipment mechanic**

Like industrial machinery mechanics, heavy equipment mechanics do not need to meet a lot of people, and they can work under their own terms.

- **Private investigator**

Being a P.I. (private investigator) was once one of the most glamorous of occupations. A P.I. can work alone and investigate without having a partner or employees.

- **HVAC mechanic**

HVAC mechanics enjoy work environments much like those of heavy equipment and industrial machinery mechanics.

- **Interpreter or translator**

Translation involves thinking and precision. You can be a verbal translator, or if you do not like speaking with and meeting people, you can translate written works.

- **Carpenter**

Carpenters earn well, and if you love woodworking you can convert your hobby into a profession.

- Heavy tractor-trailer truck driver

Truck drivers generally travel alone. You can pick up other hobbies while doing this job and still enjoying the solitude that you desire.

- **Motorboat mechanic**

This job, too, provides a lot of privacy and peace.

- **Welder**

This job is great for introverts who love peace and solitude.

- **Dental lab technician**

While this does involve meeting people, you can avoid them by concentrating on your work.

- **Motorcycle mechanic**

This is a great option for introverts who are skilled with their hands.

- **Small engine mechanic**

This is a great job option for introverts who like machines.

- **Animal trainer**

Introverts generally love spending time with animals more than humans. This is because animals cannot speak and are never judgmental.

- **Baker**

Baking is an art involving precision, thinking, and passion. If you are a great baker, why not turn your hobby into a career?

Thinking Introvert Careers

Unlike social introverts, thinking introverts do not mind social engagement. While they do not go out of their way to meet people, they don't particularly mind meeting them, either. Their energy levels do not deplete quickly after meeting other people. A major characteristic of thinking introverts is that they are highly introspective and thoughtful.

Thinking introverts have highly developed imagination and a sense of creativity. They are generally the first person to think outside the box. They can see the big picture and can bring out new ideas and innovations. Many thinking introverts are known to be good listeners. They don't just listen, but they respect other people's ideas as well. It is no wonder that thinking introverts are commonly seen in fields such as technology, engineering, art, design, etc. Some great careers for *thinking introverts* include:

- **Aerospace engineer**

This fits well for people who like to build new things and think up new ideas.

- **Environmental engineer**

This is a good option for thinking introverts who want to be innovative.

- **Industrial engineer**

This is a good option for thinking introverts who like to be bold and creative.

- **Civil engineer**

If you like planning and precision, this is a good option for you.

- **Computer programmer**

Programming needs a lot of patience and thinking. This is a highly suitable job for thinking introverts.

- **Web developer**

Like programming, web development needs a lot of patience and thinking, as well as creativity.

- **Video game artist**

If you are creative and good with art, you will reach new heights in this career field.

- **Fashion designer**

This is perfect for people who want to create new things to show off their talents.

- **Interior designer**

These people need good listening skills and patience.

- **Graphic designer**

This is a very lucrative job for introverts, as you can enjoy your privacy while working.

Anxious Introvert Jobs

Anxious introverts are like social introverts who prefer to be alone. But unlike social introverts, this desire to be alone comes from anxiety about other people and their perceptions about you. Anxious introverts are generally shy and awkward, especially in a social situation. They tend to worry a lot about their past and their future, which makes them ignore their present.

Some people may even feel weak and crippled due to their social anxiety. While there are many negatives associated with this type of introversion, there are many positives about it as well. Anxious introverts are extremely detail-oriented and love planning and precision. They are also highly focused. This makes them suitable for many different careers that call for precision, focus, and planning.

Many career options for this category include jobs that need a lot of planning and critical work. These jobs tend to be highly detail-oriented, and many involve saving people's lives. Here is a list of some of the career options that anxious introverts can take up:

- **Statistician**

Being a statistician involves a lot of precise calculations that can be difficult for others to understand.

- **Commercial pilot**

Being a commercial pilot requires immense patience and attention to detail. One wrong move can result in the deaths of hundreds of people.

- **Technical writer**

Technical writers need to be able to muster a lot of attention to avoid mistakes. This job also provides anxious introverts their much-desired solitude.

- **Accountant or auditor**

Like statisticians, these jobs need the precision required for accurate calculations.

- **Medical lab technician or technologist**

A medical lab technician needs to pay a lot of attention to the details, which is why this is a great job for anxious introverts.

- **Aircraft mechanic**

Being an aircraft mechanic requires a lot of attention to detail. It is good for people who can focus.

- Audio engineering technician

This requires the precision necessary for making minute adjustments.

- **Auto mechanic**

This requires intense precision and attention to detail.

- **Proofreader**

Reading, finding errors, and rectifying them takes a lot of focus and protracted attention. This is a great job for people who want to work in privacy.

Inhibited Introvert Careers

Inhibited introverts generally appear laid-back and very reserved. They tend to do things at their own pace. They do not like to speak or react immediately and prefer to think before they answer. They avoid making rash decisions and taking action before analysis. Inhibited introverts do not like to do anything without thinking about it a lot beforehand.

Their reserved nature and immense thinking capabilities allow these introverts to reflect upon things deeply. It also provides them a lot of observation skills and allows them to look at the big picture. Therefore, these introverts tend to do well at jobs that allow them to be the *voice of reason.*

Inhibited introverts love to think about difficult choices and questions. They do not mind big challenges, and they handle them with confidence. Ergo, many inhibited introverts work well in fields such as counseling, science, and various vocational areas. All these areas need critical thinking. Here is a list of some common career options for inhibited introverts:

- **Physicist**

Physicists need a lot of critical thinking and precision in pursuing ideas and extrapolating indicators from data.

- **Astronomer**

A great opportunity for detail-oriented introverts who like to think a lot while being alone.

- **Geoscientist**

Being a geoscientist requires a lot of research and thinking.

- **Personal financial advisor**

While it involves a certain degree of interpersonal communication, it is still recommended for an inhibited introvert.

- **Biochemist or biophysicist**

Like physicists, this job requires a lot of precise thinking.

- **Management analyst**

Management analysts must pay a lot of attention to detail and possess creativity.

- **Microbiologist**

A lot of research and precision goes into being a microbiologist.

- **Market research analyst or marketing specialist**

Understanding and predicting the trends of the market needs a lot of focused thinking.

- **Anthropologist or archaeologist**

Both fields require a lot of research and thinking.

- **Conservation scientist**

This requires a lot of focus.

- **Creative or non-fiction writer**

Writing entails a lot of thinking, creativity, and focus.

- **Wildlife biologist**

A love for animals and solitude will allow you to succeed in this career.

- **Career or education counselor**

Analyzes the life decisions of a person in a focused and precise manner.

- **Marriage or Family Therapist**

Analyzes the intricate details of marriage and the married life of the couple.

- **Mental health counselor**

These counselors must remember much detail in order to help others properly.

- **Addictions counselor**

Being an addictions counselor requires a lot of thinking and focus on helping people.

Chapter Eighteen: The Introverted Leader

Why Introverts Make Great Leaders

For decades, people have believed that introverts cannot be great and capable leaders because they do not possess those qualities needed for leadership. People believed that introverts are incapable and ineffective, and their possessing a leadership style is just not plausible.

This myth has percolated to the top of the business world. In fact, more than 65% of senior executives in the western world believe that introversion is a bad sign for business-oriented teammates. They believe that only 6% of introverts can take over huge companies and manage a team successfully. Many businessmen believe that leaders need to possess certain qualities such as gregariousness, outgoing nature, and expert networking skills to be successful. As these skills are generally perceived to be inherent in extroverts and generally lacking in introverts, many leaders dismiss introverts out-of-hand when considering candidates for leadership positions. This is obviously a myth and a nonsensical position.

What Is an Introvert?

Introverts and extroverts, as terms, were first introduced by Carl Jung in the 1920s. Introverts are people who tend to get their energy from time spent alone rather than in socializing. Extroverts tend to get their energy from socializing. Introverts are generally introspective and quiet. They are often observant, but sometimes shy.

Some people believe that introverts and extroverts are like opposite poles and that there is a wide difference between the two types, but this is not true; true introverts and true extroverts do not exist. People tend to be somewhere towards the middle of the spectrum in both these personality types.

Introverts are often written off as antisocial people who do not like talking to people or being around them. This is, of course, false. Introverts are not necessarily anti-social. They prefer solitude because they like to contemplate and think over matters that are important to them. They feel rejuvenated and refreshed when they have time alone, allowing them to look at things from a new and different perspective. Many people hold to the myth that being an introvert means that you are a loser and that you are an awkward nerd. But this is a myth; introverts *do* like to spend time with other people – just on *their own terms.*

As said above, no one is thoroughly extroverted or introverted. But according to an estimate, around 33-55% of people are skewed towards introversion. But this demographic changes drastically once we enter the world of business. In the corporate world, more than 96% of people are extroverted. The number is even higher when the topmost positions are considered as a category, showing that there is a strong prejudice against introverts in the world of business. Many leaders rank extroversion as the best trait that a leader can have. This bias against introversion is not only harmful to introverts, but it also harmful to the business world itself. Due to this bias, the world of business has lost countless great leaders who could have changed the world!

While it is now generally accepted that there is a bias against introverts in the world of business, the question is, what is the reason behind this bias? To find the answer to the problem, let's consider the history behind it.

How Culture Defines "Leadership"

The definitions of "leader" and "leadership" vary, but in simple cultural terms, leadership is the process through which other people are influenced in such a way that they work together to achieve a common goal of the group.

In the beginning, leaders were meant to be people who encouraged their team members to work collectively toward the team goals. But with time, the definition changed, and now leaders are singular, charismatic, bold titans who rule their teams. In this paradigm, the leader's team-building skills are not as important as managing the team's public image.

There are dozens of studies throughout the last century aimed at finding out what traits make good leaders. If the results of these tests and studies are taken cumulatively, the traits mentioned in the studies are present in both personality types, and some are perhaps seen more in introverts than extroverts. None of the traits go against the typical behavior and attitude of introverts, so it is a curious case as to why introverts are still not being offered leadership positions. The answer to this problem is perhaps the myths that surround introversion and leadership. Let us have a look at these myths one by one.

• Myth #1: Introverts do not like leadership roles

This is one of the most perpetuated myths about introverts, and it is clearly false. Introverts do want to be leaders; *they just do not get the chance to do so.*

Introverts are present and have succeeded in almost all walks of life, be it sports, arts, business, movies, music, or politics. Many famous leaders in these fields who were introverts include Audrey Hepburn, Michael Jordan, Mahatma Gandhi, and Albert Einstein. Many important presidents of the United States of America, including Abraham Lincoln, Thomas Jefferson, and Barack Obama, were introverts. Even in the world of business, many prominent leaders, including Mark Zuckerberg, Bill Gates, and Warren Buffet, are introverts. This proves that introverts are present and successful at leading in all fields.

Introverts can do well in any field; they just need to learn how to use their skills properly. Instead of keeping their talents and skills hidden, introverts should tap into them. Many introverted traits that are generally looked down upon in the world of business can prove to be beneficial.

- Myth #2: Introverts don't have the "people skills"

Another myth that is popular in the world of business is that introverts do not possess "people skills". This means that they do not possess the skills such as confidence and charisma that are necessary for effective leadership.

Recent research found that while it is indeed more likely that a charming individual will be hired as a CEO, his or her charm does not guarantee his or her success and performance. This means that charm has nothing to do with performance. In the same study, it was observed that introverted leaders did far better than leaders who were hired just for their charming personalities.

It is true that introverted leaders are generally not as cheerful or bubbly as an extroverted leader, but their lack of cheerfulness does not correlate to their leadership skills. Introverted leaders are generally more in tune with their senses and thus can read the emotional cues of people with ease.

The frontal area of the brains of introverts is highly active. This area contains the frontal lobes and the thalamus, areas responsible for various problem solving and thinking activities; therefore, introverted leaders are actually better equipped for making the appropriate decisions even in a time of crisis.

- **Myth #3: Introverts are bad communicators**

Many people often get confused by the way introverts process their ideas differently from extroverts. Many times, this internal processing of ideas can be confusing to extroverts. They may even misjudge introverts and think that they are not interested in the situation. Introverts are methodical thinkers who like to think properly. They tend to go over different scenarios in their minds before coming to a decision. This allows them to be sure of their plans. Once they are sure of their plans, they communicate them to people with full confidence. This is a great way of communicating with people. It is also highly suitable for leadership positions. This allows introverts to present their ideas in a more concrete, well-thought-out, and lucid manner.

- **Myth #4: Introverts don't like collaborating**

It is true that introverts prefer to work alone and that they are highly productive when they are left to their own devices. This does not mean that they cannot work properly on a team, or that they are unable to lead people toward a collaborative goal. Introverted leaders can be especially good in difficult situations.

A study conducted at Harvard University found that extroverted leaders are great for passive teams, but they can be quite problematic for proactive teams. In the latter case, all members of the team are treated equally, and the ideas of all the team members are accepted. Introverts are far more suitable for such teams. As introverts are known for their listening skills, they can help such teams to achieve greater success. Introverts are more receptive to other people's ideas.

Tips for Introverted Leaders

It should now be clear that introverts can become very good leaders. That said, convincing others might take some time. But don't worry, you can move on vigilantly and keep pushing on, determined and confident. Self-confidence is the key to winning big in life.

Many tips can help you become a great introverted leader. In this section, let us have a look at some of these tips one by one.

- **Listen first, talk later**

This is a natural tendency of introverts. Introverts tend to listen a lot more than speak. It is a great skill that can be used in the world of business. If you want to be known and respected as a great leader, you should always pay attention to what other people are saying. You need to listen to what your clients, friends, employees, and followers are trying to tell you. It does not matter who is the best speaker, because the best talkers generally do not have the best ideas.

- **Step up during times of crisis**

Crises and problems are a common part of everyone's life. We all face personal and professional crises from time to time. It does not matter how many crises you face; what matters most is how you face them, and how you respond to things in a time of adversity. A leader needs to be the voice of reason all the time. Even if the ship is sinking, a leader needs to motivate people to save the day. Introverts are blessed with good thinking skills and patience. These two skills are essential in the time of crisis.

- **Get out of your complacent zone**

As explained in a previous chapter, you need to learn how to get out of your complacent zone. If you want to be a leader, you will have to get out of your comfort zone ever so slightly but leave your complacency zone behind. Being a leader involves talking to people and managing them. While you may not like talking to people, if you want to be a successful leader, you will have to do so. Even if you believe that small talk is worthless and hate it, you will still have to do it from time to time. If you find public speaking especially difficult, take a public speaking class. Take the lead on new projects and volunteer to take on new things. Work on yourself every day and move forward gradually. Each week should bring in a new day of personal success for you.

- **Get into your comfort zone**

Introverts love to talk to themselves and think about things. These two things are crucial, along with solitude, for introverts. These sessions allow them to mull things over and relax. A relaxed brain can look at things from various points of view and produce excellent ideas and solutions. So, as a leader, always set some time aside for yourself. It does not need to be an hour; you can even take a 15-minute break and sit alone quietly. Let your thoughts flow and let your body relax completely. If you get any ideas while doing this, don't get up until the session is over. Once the session is over, you can move on to the next tip.

- **Write it down**

Introverts are generally better writers than speakers. This is why you should put your ideas on paper as much as possible before speaking about them. Take some key points and highlight them. This will help you speak clearly and lucidly. Always leave employees with challenging questions, as that will help them perform better.

You may have noticed that certain traits are common in introverts as well as extroverts. Introverts can use their strengths, such as listening and observation skills, to become excellent leaders. If you believe that you have some weaknesses, accept them, and try to work on them. This way, you will become a great leader.

Chapter Nineteen: How Introverts Can Change the World

Responsible citizens of the world who feel that they owe something to society and humanity, often dream of changing the world. They want to make it a better place. Such people want to bring positive changes to the lives of other people. If you are one such person, you want to see the world from a positive point of view. You want people to remember you as a trailblazer and a reformer who changed the lives of people for the greater good. While all of this is quite easy for extroverts, thanks to their outgoing and sociable natures, it can seem quite difficult for introverts, especially if you are one of those people who dislikes even the thought of going out. But this does not mean that you cannot make a difference in the lives of people. It is still possible.

If you are a highly introverted and socially awkward person who wants to change the world but does not know how to start, don't worry; you are not alone. There are many people like you, and there is hope. In this chapter, you will find many tips and suggestions that you can use to learn how to change the world, one step at a time.

Do Most of the Work by Yourself

Introverts do not mind people, but they would rather do things on their own. This is because introverts prefer solitude, and they like to do things at their own pace and while enjoying their own space. If you really want to change the world, understand your pros and tackle your cons.

Changing the world does not mean that you need to get out of the house and organize protests, sit-ins, and marches. You can change the world right from your home. Try to find methods that can help you support the world-changing movements going on outside of your comfort zone. For instance, if people need clothes, you can help them by creating clothing items in your home.

Leave Your Creations as Legacy

Introverts are generally blessed artists. If you are talented and have artistic skills, you can use them to change the world. There are many ways through which you can use art to change the world. Massive conceptual street art installations, photojournalism, or writing thought-pieces are all great avenues by which to leave your mark. If you want to be more local, then arrange art pieces that will connect with the local audience. This way, you will be able to make a difference that you will be able to observe immediately.

If You Do Interact with People, Interact via the Written Word

Introverts are not always great with verbal communication, but they are generally good with written communication. Many writers and famous authors were introverts. If you feel overwhelmed at the prospect of talking to people to change the world, don't worry. Instead of forcing yourself to do something that you find unpleasant, choose methods that will help you achieve the same goals without discomforting you. Instead of delivering speeches in marches, write columns and articles. Your writing can motivate others to move ahead and take things into their own hands. Thus, you will be able to lead a revolution without having to get out of your comfort zone.

Scout Your Surroundings

If you decide to use your art for public demonstration, it's best to scout the area thoroughly before choosing a place to put up your art. This way, you will know how many people will be able to check out your art. Introverts do not like crowds, but if you want to change the world, you need to attract a significant number of people towards your piece.

It's OK to Fail or Avoid Certain Ideas

Introverts like to think a lot, which is why they arrive at exceptional ideas. Many times, it is difficult to make these ideas real. You may dream of making documentaries and art pieces that will change the world (and win good awards), but it does not happen all the time.

Just being an introvert does not mean that you will get ideas that are only suitable for your personality. Many times, introverts get ideas that are far better suited to extroverts. In such cases, introverts rarely act upon these ideas, and the ideas die out. This is because the hustle and bustle involved in bringing these ideas to fruition are taxing, if not impossible to bear, for introverts.

This doesn't mean that you should not think of ambitious ideas. You may feel scared of them now, but times may change, and you may pursue them successfully in the future. If you believe that your idea is too big and scary, try breaking it into chunks and doing it step by step. Or, you can put the big idea aside and start with smaller and simpler ideas instead. Taking small steps and succeeding is far better than taking big steps and failing.

Embrace the Awkward

If you are socially awkward along with being an introvert, don't worry, and instead of hiding your awkwardness, embrace it. Use your awkwardness in a way that will help you send a message to people. Being awkward and feeling awkward is not a negative thing. Rather, it is a sign of growth and development. If you feel awkward doing something, it means that you are doing something that you are not comfortable with. If you feel self-conscious while helping someone, don't worry. Carry on, and soon you will stop feeling strange.

Don't Use Your Introversion as an Excuse

It does not matter whether you are an introvert or an extrovert; anyone can change the world if he or she has the dedication and passion. Instead of blaming your introversion for your inaction, sit down and contemplate why you are not taking any action to change the world. Often, you will find reasons that are not at all related to your introversion. Instead of hiding your introverted characteristics, use them and turn them into assets.

Being an introvert can make a huge difference if you know how to use it. To change the world, you need to act, and to act, you need to get out of your complacent zone. Treat this as a personal growth exercise. If you try to change things for good, you will soon notice them changing. That said, you must try first. If you accept defeat even before trying, then you will never succeed!

So, ultimately, if you want to change the world, change yourself. Make the effort, being bold and confident. Take baby steps if you are not comfortable making huge changes in your own life. With time, you will surely be able to make a difference in the world.

Conclusion

I am sure by now it is clear to you how difficult and confusing an introvert's life can be. It is full of contradictions and complex situations. It is no wonder that introverts tend to stay away from crowds and social gatherings, as those groups are extremely *extrovert* friendly!

One of the most important things that every introvert needs to remember is that introversion is perfectly normal. Many introverts try to change themselves and put a lot of pressure on their brains to become an extrovert. Instead of trying to change, it is better to accept who you are and use your characteristics as assets. If you accept your qualities, you can use them for your benefit.

This book contained many tips and tricks that may help you lead a comfortable introverted life. These tips are tried and tested, and they work. It is recommended that you practice them frequently so that they become habits, allowing you to use them in a far more natural way.

Remember, always be confident and bold, and have patience. Be yourself, and the world will love you.

References

https://www.learning-mind.com/4-introvert-types-which-one-are-you/

https://thriveglobal.com/stories/25-signs-that-tell-you-are-an-introvert%EF%BB%BF/

https://www.mindfulnessmuse.com/individual-differences/myers-briggs-8-introverted-personality-types

https://introvertdear.com/what-it-feels-like-to-be-an-introvert/

https://introvertspring.com/15-introvert-myths-busted/

https://www.elegantthemes.com/blog/business/famous-introverts-and-what-you-can-learn-from-them

http://www.magicaldaydream.com/2015/09/7-tips-on-how-to-change-the-world-if-youre-an-introverted-unicorn.html

https://thehustle.co/why-introverts-make-great-leaders/

https://www.lifehack.org/articles/communication/5-simple-and-effective-leadership-tips-for-introverts.html

https://www.scienceofpeople.com/introvert/

https://www.trade-schools.net/articles/best-jobs-for-introverts.asp

https://psych2go.net/10-things-introverts-need-relationship/

https://psych2go.net/6-relationship-tips-for-introverts/

https://www.huffpost.com/entry/how-to-network-introvert_l_5d13d8c2e4b0d0a2c0ab3e92

https://www.forbes.com/sites/jonlevy/2018/04/20/8-networking-tips-for-introverts-from-a-superconnector/#60845ca226ef https://introvertdear.com/news/introverts-guide-making-friends-get/

https://www.valgeisler.com/11-perfectly-introverted-ways-to-make-friends-as-an-adult/

https://introvertspring.com/how-to-make-friends-if-youre-an-introvert/

https://www.quietrev.com/the-4-differences-between-introversion-and-social-anxiety/

https://themighty.com/2019/03/introvert-with-social-anxiety-what-to-know/

https://www.elitedaily.com/p/how-introverts-can-make-small-talk-less-painful-more-meaningful-according-to-experts-8917603

https://www.lifehack.org/articles/lifestyle/7-epic-strategies-for-introverts-by-introverts-to-ignite-your-social-skills.html

http://elitemanmagazine.com/10-tips-to-becoming-more-social-as-an-introvert/

https://www.wikihow.com/Be-Socially-Confident

https://introvertdear.com/news/anxious-introverts-fears/

https://psych2go.net/5-steps-to-overcome-your-fears-as-an-introvert/

https://introvertdear.com/news/introverts-happy-need/

https://www.verywellmind.com/how-to-be-a-happy-introvert-1717557

https://introvertdear.com/news/introverts-alone-time-science-marti-olsen-laney/

https://psychcentral.com/lib/introverts-and-the-quest-for-quiet/

https://blog.dropbox.com/topics/work-culture/introverts-quiet-time-creativity

https://introvertspring.com/the-truth-about-introvert-anxiety-and-depression/

https://www.familyaddictionspecialist.com/blog/how-mental-health-issues-may-differ-among-introverts-and-extroverts

https://introvertdear.com/news/5-reasons-introverts-mental-health-plan/

https://jenniferrabin.com/introverts-can-change-world/

Part 2: Social Anxiety

Discover How to Quiet Your Negative Thoughts, Overcome Worry, Build Your Social Skills, and Cure Shyness so You Can Have Small Talk with Ease Even as an Introvert

SOCIAL ANXIETY

DISCOVER HOW TO QUIET YOUR NEGATIVE THOUGHTS, OVERCOME WORRY, BUILD YOUR SOCIAL SKILLS, AND CURE SHYNESS SO YOU CAN HAVE SMALL TALK WITH EASE EVEN AS AN INTROVERT

DARON CALLAWAY

Introduction

The times we're living in are unprecedented in many ways, and yet, deep down, we have hardly changed for thousands of years. What this means is that our lifestyle, technology, and many other things that shape our days have, in a way, surpassed us. Modern living certainly provides many comforts and perks; still, we often find ourselves naturally unequipped to deal with some of the challenges that these new ways of life have brought with them.

Some of the problems that used to be a freak occurrence - and only bothered particularly unfortunate individuals - are now becoming more commonplace. These problems include numerous forms of personality disorders and other mental health concerns, one of which is social anxiety. It is a sad and strange irony that social anxiety is an increasingly common problem in a time when our means of communication are more advanced and accessible than ever - *and when the world is interconnected like never before.*

Indeed, many folks from all walks of life seem to struggle with social interaction nowadays, so you're far from being alone. Social interaction is one of the critical aspects of the human experience, which is why social anxiety can not only deprive you of pleasant moments but also make your professional life suffer significantly. Folks who don't have such problems might not even realize it, but social interaction permeates a normal human life as few other things do. Getting even the most menial of tasks done can entail interaction, and when that becomes difficult, life can really take a downward turn.

Seeing as we are such social animals by nature, social skills are also one of the more important predictors of success. It's no secret that those who are adept at social situations tend to get ahead in many areas of life, especially when it comes to career opportunities and romantic prospects. Overall, social skills are one of the most critical areas to improve for a more fulfilled life.

The objective of this book is to help you do exactly that. If you have experience with social anxiety or suspect that you might, this book will teach you precisely what this disorder is and how it works, but also how you can mend the problem. Indeed, even though it's a complex issue that's still being researched, social anxiety is something that you can fight on your own, with moderate to great success.

It's important to understand that you are only one of many people with this problem and that there's nothing inherently wrong with you. Social anxiety can have numerous causes, but the cure is almost always the same or very similar. In the simplest possible terms, the issue revolves around a skill that you've lost and will have to master again. In the process, you will also master yourself.

By the end of this book, you will have a better understanding of what this disorder truly is, but you will also know much more about how exactly your brain works, particularly in relation to social anxiety. You will learn to differentiate between social anxiety and some other normal psychological processes or personality traits like introversion, fear, or plain old shyness.

While it's not a substitute for professional psychiatric help and therapy, this book contains up-to-date information and proven methods to overcome your anxiety. It will also help you on your journey toward greater self-development and awareness, both of which are important for achieving long-lasting peace of mind. In the process of overcoming your anxiety, you will become a more confident individual and will learn valuable skills in communication.

No matter how many bad experiences you've had and however hopeless your situation might feel, you are not beyond help. As you will find in this book, beating your social anxiety might be difficult, and it might feel like an uphill battle at times, which is why you'll need patience and perseverance, on top of a desire to get better. Nonetheless, it is a battle that every person has the strength to win. That strength must be unlocked, though, and this book will eventually help you do that. Without further ado, we will begin by looking at what social anxiety really is and where we are at when it comes to an understanding and treating this problem.

Chapter One: What Is Social Anxiety?

It is important to state that social anxiety is not merely shyness or introversion, although they might often correlate. Social anxiety is a diagnosed personality disorder, generally referred to as social anxiety disorder, or SAD for short. Social anxiety was formerly known as social phobia, which is a term that's still sometimes used. In the simplest terms, social anxiety is a sort of fear of social situations that stems from a feeling of inadequacy and a fear of being scrutinized in some way.

Everyone can get nervous about certain situations, particularly when they are important. For instance, many people tend to get nervous before an important job interview, even if they don't really have a social anxiety disorder. And even though this nervousness usually comes from the fear of scrutiny that a job interview will inevitably entail, it's still not social anxiety disorder *by definition*. Social anxiety implies a particularly intense and irrational fear that can completely cloud your mind and occurs automatically - even when you can't rationally identify what it is about a situation that scares you. The irrationality and intensity of the fearful reaction that social anxiety entails are why it's sometimes referred to as a social phobia.

The fact that we have evolved to be social creatures is something that makes social anxiety particularly tragic and problematic. Even when we have such a disorder and when our fear makes us think that we don't want to get into social situations, our minds still subtly crave the interaction and the contact. Prolonged isolation and a lack of intimacy or any social contact, however meaningful or not, can have dramatic consequences on our mental health, regardless of how sociable or unsociable, we think we are.

Of course, therefore, social anxiety often leads to feelings of loneliness and alienation. As you might know from experience, this is a difficult situation to be in because it feels like an awfully paradoxical trap where one loathes the prospect of getting into a social situation but feels the same way about their loneliness in the meantime. As such, a social anxiety disorder can lead to all sorts of complications when it comes to mental or even physical health, depending on the case. That's if the disorder is left unchecked, of course.

If you have only a moderate problem with social anxiety, you should certainly try to nip it in the bud. At this time, you might think that it only affects your social life and makes it difficult to make friends, but, over time, social anxiety can make many other areas of your life difficult, as we mentioned. If the problem can grow, you can find yourself going from feeling discomfort at a party to having your career stifled, or worse.

Seeing as it can have such far-reaching consequences for the quality of life and productivity of individuals, it's no surprise that social anxiety disorder is something that's of great concern for society. SAD (social anxiety disorder) is just one of the numerous forms of anxiety disorders that pose a problem, particularly in the West. In the United States, anxiety disorders affect some 40 million adults, making such disorders the most common form of mental health issue. On a yearly basis, around one-fifth of adult Americans will report being affected by some form of anxiety.

The incidence of social anxiety disorder is around 7% of the adult population in the US. This statistic includes mild to severe cases of social anxiety, but it only accounts for individuals with a prolonged problem. Folks who are affected by SAD for shorter periods of time are even more numerous. Since it affects millions of people, social anxiety has its cost for the economy as well, just like other forms of anxiety. Because it's a growing problem across the board, social anxiety now receives significant attention, and we understand it much better than we used to.

Symptoms

Social anxiety – a diagnosed disease - comes with a range of identifiable symptoms that can be used to determine if the issue is SAD or if it is something else. Of course, the symptoms of social anxiety are mostly like those of other forms of anxiety disorders, while the main difference is in the triggers that bring those symptoms. The symptoms can generally be divided into emotional or behavioral symptoms and physical symptoms.

Indeed, when it strikes, social anxiety can interfere with the way you behave in certain situations and how you feel both physically and emotionally. However, when it comes to behavior, social anxiety has long-term, persistent symptoms and signs as well. It alters one's lifestyle, habits, plans, and eventually, even life outcomes. When it comes to the behavioral and emotional side of things, below are some of the common symptoms and signs of social anxiety disorder:

- Excessive fear of judgment and social situations that might lead to it
- The fear of communicating with strangers
- Obsessing over the possibility of embarrassing yourself or being publically humiliated
- The fear of anxiety itself or, rather, of others noticing the problem or its physical symptoms that you might be experiencing

- The fear of attracting the attention of others, especially in groups or crowds
- Persistent and sometimes growing anxiety in anticipation of an upcoming social situation that you're aware of in advance
- Adjusting plans and canceling activities to avoid triggers, even at the detriment to your social or professional life
- Ceasing to partake in activities that used to bring you pleasure and joy, simply for fear of social situations and the anxiety they bring
- Obsessive posthoc analysis of every detail of interaction after it has ended, with a focus on how you performed during its course
- An inability to focus on the other party in a conversation, instead of obsessing over your own appearance and behavior
- An excessively negative outlook on future social scenarios and their consequences

Because of all these issues, folks with social anxiety tend to struggle with starting conversations, participating in group activities, meeting strangers, dating, maintaining eye contact, visiting a store, or even using a public restroom. When an outbreak of social anxiety occurs, you will usually notice the following symptoms:

- An increased heart rate - *sometimes, severely so*
- Trembling
- Stress sweating
- Nausea
- Blushing
- Trouble breathing, which can make it difficult to speak as well
- Dizziness
- An overall loss of control over your thoughts and a feeling of panic

If you tend to experience any or all these symptoms in social situations and are made to feel very uncomfortable because of it, this is a good indication that you're struggling with a social anxiety disorder.

Diagnosis and Complications

As we mentioned, social anxiety disorder has been taken seriously by mainstream psychiatry and psychology for quite a while now, especially in the developed world. As such, it is a disorder that can be diagnosed with great accuracy. Analyzing the symptoms after they have occurred and been observed is one way of diagnosis, but experts have also developed useful questionnaires and personality tests that can evaluate whether you have SAD and how severe it might be.

If you decide to talk to a professional in order to confirm beyond any doubt whether you have a social anxiety disorder, you might be asked to talk about past symptoms or take a questionnaire. The questionnaires usually consist of statements that you are supposed to agree or disagree with. Such tests can vary in complexity, but their core idea is to get insight into the way you react to certain situations and how your mind works. The results will then help determine whether you are socially anxious - and to what degree.

In addition to considering the symptoms and signs we have already discussed, you can also take such tests and quizzes on your own. There are all sorts of quizzes that you can find on the Internet, some more detailed and reliable than others. Still, the most accurate diagnosis will require consulting with a professional who will be able to consider all the particularities of your individual case.

If left unchecked, a social anxiety disorder can evolve in many ways and lead to complications, especially when it comes to your overall mental health. In time, your social anxiety can take charge of every aspect of your life, dictating everything you do and how or when you do it. Socially anxious people often end up with diminished self-esteem and, of course, abysmal social skills. These problems are especially likely when the onset of the disorder is during the teenage years, which is an important developmental stage. Unfortunately, this scenario is all too common when it comes to SAD, and kids can thus miss out on developing crucial social skills and confidence that will come into play later in life.

Social anxiety can make people fragile and irritable, unable to handle criticism or even take friendly advice. Folks with SAD tend to be much less assertive as well, which hinders professional and academic performance. As the disorder pushes the individual further into isolation, all sorts of other problems can come up. It's not uncommon for socially anxious individuals to end up with major depressive disorder and many other mental issues that can even lead to suicide – or, at least, attempts of it. Of course, many sufferers will also resort to self-medicating with alcohol or drugs, which, in turn, can lead to substance abuse and a whole plethora of other problems that go along with that.

Causes and Risk Factors

As is often the case with these things, the causes of social anxiety disorder can vary, and they are worth discussion. Overall, social anxiety disorder stems from biological or environmental factors or a combination of both. It has been observed that social anxiety is often inherited, but it's unclear whether this heritability stems from genetics or nurture and learned behavior. It's certainly possible that social anxiety, like other mental problems, can be passed down through genes, but this is still debated.

As for the brain itself, it has been suggested that the party responsible for the fearful and anxious reaction is the amygdala. When this part of the brain is abnormally active, which is the case in some people, social anxiety tends to be a problem.

When it comes to the environmental factors that might cause the disorder, they are plentiful. Past experiences can play an important role, particularly negative social experiences. They can be especially affecting if they occur when one is very young or otherwise vulnerable. Of course, parents can also be the inadvertent culprits either by setting an example with their own anxious behavior or by being overprotective or not properly socializing their child during the formative years. As for direct mistreatment or child abuse, it's unclear if such experiences in childhood can lead to social anxiety, although they are certainly connected to other problems.

Apart from the murky and debated subject of underlying causes, there are also risk factors to consider, all of which can imply a higher risk of developing SAD at some point in life. Apart from family history and the parental influence we mentioned, environmental risk factors for children also include experiences like bullying, excessive teasing, humiliation, and failure to make friends. Such experiences can lead to withdrawal and alienation, greatly contributing to subsequent social anxiety. Children who exhibit traits like shyness and a lack of sociability early in their lives should be worked with to reduce their elevated risk of developing SAD.

In the unfortunate cases where people have a condition or an appearance problem that attracts attention, the risk of social anxiety is higher as well. This includes many things that can make us self-conscious and turn social interaction into a chore, even if the people we interact with are kind to us. One of the most common problems of this kind is acne. Acne's onset during teenage years often correlates with the emergence of social anxiety, and it can certainly make things worse.

Treatment

Today, social anxiety is something that's treated with much success, and the chances are good that treatment options will get even better in the future. The two main approaches are cognitive-behavioral therapy – "CBT" for short - and medication. Of course, therapy will also often make use of both approaches, depending on the case in question.

Cognitive-behavioral therapy is an approach that focuses on the patient's thought patterns and other mental processes, considering how they affect anxiety. You will find later that this book's advice essentially constitutes CBT as well. It's simply the idea that by altering the patient's way of thinking via the use of counseling and personalized therapy, the patient can abandon thoughts and beliefs that lead to social anxiety. By changing thoughts and behavior, CBT truly addresses the root cause of the problem.

As its name suggests, CBT consists of two parts, wherein the cognitive part of the therapy deals with thoughts, and the behavioral half focuses on various activities. When it comes to CBT that's specific to social anxiety treatment, the cognitive part of the therapy tends to focus on replacing negative thoughts that trigger anxiety with positive ones. The behavioral component of the therapy often includes group therapy that involves activities that are meant to condition the patient to tolerate certain situations better gradually.

These activities tend to be those that have the potential to be at least somewhat uncomfortable for the patient, but it's a process of slow immunization, so to speak. Furthermore, group therapy activities provide an opportunity to put into practice the things a patient learns during cognitive therapy. This is one of the reasons why CBT is such a comprehensive and effective approach. CBT might also make use of relaxation techniques like meditation, mindfulness, and other approaches - many of which we will cover later in this book.

When it comes to meditation, if it's possible to treat the disorder without medication successfully, and although that's *ideal* (medication can indeed be very helpful), the medication that's used to treat social anxiety is what you would expect with other forms of anxiety as well, including benzodiazepines and SSRIs. The two main problems with medication are that they have side-effects and that they only treat the symptoms instead of addressing the *root cause.* That's why medication is only an additional tool to make the journey easier, not a long-term solution.

All in all, therapy for social anxiety has a great success rate, and in almost all cases, the problem is curable. Once the mind has been altered for the better and taught to look at things in a new light, the positive change is usually permanent. Often, all it takes is some willpower and patience on your part, as you'll see throughout this book.

Chapter Two: Social Anxiety, Shyness, and Introversion

In this chapter, we will go into more detail concerning the differences and connection between social anxiety and a couple of things that might resemble the disorder or accompany it but may also exist without SAD. First and foremost, it's important to understand that one's level of comfort in social situations, especially when we account for various personal preferences, can depend on many factors other than disorders or any kind of illness. Being a bit on the shy side is certainly a legitimate personality trait and not any kind of disorder.

Furthermore, being shy or anxious in certain social situations can be entirely natural, even for people who are otherwise never shy. Talking to a person you really like or being in a situation with strangers while noticing something sketchy going on can make anyone feel anxious and on edge. As you probably know, some people are also just naturally predisposed to being more outgoing and communicative than others, and sociability is certainly a spectrum. Understanding what shyness and introversion are, for instance, can be just as useful as knowing the symptoms that we discussed earlier when it comes to identifying social anxiety.

Introversion

To start with, let's look at what being an introvert truly means. In one of the later chapters, we will carefully consider a list of situations and settings that can be difficult for introverts, with or without social anxiety. For now, we'll stick to brass tacks. In practical terms, an introvert is a person who likes calm and relatively quiet environments and settings that aren't overly stimulating. While they might not scare the introvert, such situations can be mentally and emotionally draining for them, which is why introverts usually need a period of relaxation in solitude after a prolonged period of socializing. The more stimulating and intense that socialization is, the more of an effect it will have.

The concepts of introversion and extroversion in humans can be traced back to one of the most famous psychologists, Carl Jung, who introduced these terms in 1921. In its essence, this whole concept didn't primarily focus on sociability. Rather, Jung postulated that an introvert is simply someone who is more focused on and more attuned to their inner thoughts and feelings. It's a sort of inward focus characterized by things like frequent introspection and a focus on everything inside themselves. On the other hand, an extrovert is a person who focuses primarily or exclusively on the outside world.

Jung's theory later played an important party in other theories of personality, such as the "Big Five" theory, also known as the five-factor model. This is essentially a system of grouping personality traits, and it's still used today. Another well-known instance of the use of the introvert-extrovert scale is the Myers-Briggs Type Indicator or MBTI. This is a system and test that has been used for a while now to categorize people into pre-defined personality types, and an individual's introversion or extroversion plays an important role in that.

Over time, these terms have evolved, and various psychologists have given their contribution to evolving the definitions. Today, it's quite clear to us that introverts also tend to be less sociable than extroverts, although, once again, they aren't necessarily socially anxious or even shy. When it comes to social or any other kinds of stimulation coming from the outside, extroverts tend not just to prefer but also need more of it. For instance, whereas an extrovert might need to go out to a party in the evening and engage with a lot of people to feel fulfilled, an introvert will usually prefer to sit at someone's home with two or three close friends and have a laid-back, quiet evening. All in all, introverts will focus on their internal feelings while extroverts focus on external stimulation.

All of this is best viewed as a spectrum between extroversion and introversion, meaning that there are few folks who are extremely introverted or extroverted. Most people are somewhere on the middle ground, but a lean toward one or the other is certainly apparent in most people. It's impossible to know the exact figure, but it is estimated that folks who can be defined as introverted account for some 25 to 40% of the population.

While social anxiety is, as we discussed, a disorder most likely caused by a combination of genetic and environmental factors, it's even less clear what causes introversion. On top of that, introversion is in no way considered a disorder. There are, of course, some proposed explanations. In general, introverts and extroverts are most likely born that way, but environmental factors can certainly play a part. After all, it's difficult to determine how exactly your personality forms. The important thing to understand is that introversion is perfectly normal and natural.

The key difference between social anxiety and introversion is that the former implies fear, while the latter is all about preference. While introversion is simply a way you live, social anxiety is something that keeps you from living. Furthermore, while the cause is broad, the inner workings of introversion and extroversion are well understood. A study published a few years ago in Frontiers in Human Neuroscience by Richard Depue and co-authors at the College of Human Ecology has given us more insight in this regard.

According to the researchers, introversion and extroversion have a lot to do with the way in which the reward system in an individual's brain works. It basically boils down to brain chemistry, notably dopamine. In the simplest terms, dopamine is a chemical that your brain releases to give you a rewarding sensation whenever you succeed at something or acquire a thing that you want. In the brains of extroverts, researchers say, there is a much higher and more stimulating response to dopamine. Because of this, extroverts are more motivated to seek out higher stimulation, which inevitably makes them more outgoing.

The Marks of an Introvert

You will learn more about how to differentiate between social anxiety and things like introversion as we proceed, but for now, let us look at some common signs of introversion. As you can probably gather by now, while there is a high correlation between introversion and slower social life, that doesn't mean that introverts can't be quite sociable. This is why performance in social situations is not always a reliable indicator. A much better indicator of introversion and extroversion is how an individual performs in solitude.

Solitude isn't really stimulating, which is why extroverts have a particularly difficult time dealing with it. If you find it easy or even preferable to spend time alone, that's a strong indicator of introversion. Do you find yourself enjoying a quiet evening at home with some hot chocolate and a book much more than a big party? Do you prefer small, quiet gatherings with a select few friends or relatives? These are signs that you are probably an introvert.

However, if you often find yourself incredibly bored, restless, and frustrated when you are alone, then you might be an extrovert. The thing is, however, that if you feel like this when alone but still struggle and feel incredibly uncomfortable in social situations, then this is a very good indicator that your problem is a social anxiety disorder. This would be a clear case of fear over preference, as we mentioned earlier. You find yourself craving interaction and the stimulation that it brings, but you struggle with it, and that's when the problem goes beyond the matter of introversion and extroversion.

The reason why introverts will often feel that their energy has been drained after a while of socializing is not that they are necessarily unsociable, but because of their different response to stimulation. Consider how you feel after you go to a party or a large family gathering. Do you feel drained and worn out or recharged? Indeed, while social situations drain the introvert's energy, they recharge the extrovert.

Another common sign of introversion is deep and sophisticated introspection. If you tend to spend a lot of your waking hours in introspection, listening to your inner voice, daydreaming, and otherwise disregarding the world around you, then you are almost certainly an introvert. We already mentioned that introverts are characterized by a focus on their inner feelings, but that doesn't mean they're just more emotional. It has to do with the way introverts process all the input they receive from the outside world. The extrovert tends to perceive things externally while the introvert will internalize the information and process it through their intricate inner conversations and feelings.

All of this implies a high level of self-awareness, which might be the reason why introverts are more likely to be self-conscious and, in turn, socially anxious. Introverts tend to know themselves rather well, meaning that they are in touch with their emotions and understand their own motivations, thoughts, and ideas. If you're an introvert, this might seem like nothing special to you, but the truth is that a lot of people struggle with understanding what and why they feel most of the time or even why they do certain things. Introverts usually don't have that problem. In general, if you spend a lot of time soul-searching and trying to get to the bottom of your thoughts, you are likely introverted.

Introverts also can concentrate on things very closely, especially on one task at a time. If you prefer to maintain focus on one thing at a time instead of multitasking, that's a sign of introversion. Furthermore, when it comes to learning how to do a certain job or absorbing a new skill, introverts will usually prefer to learn through observation for a while before getting into the mix. This often entails learning from others by watching them perform. Extroverts tend to rely more on trial and error.

Introverts also like autonomy, particularly at work. It's not that introverts can't function as part of a team, but if they are given a choice, they tend to prefer jobs that provide them a dose of independence or even isolation. Not only would an introvert prefer such a job, but they tend to perform better on them as well.

Another clue you can look for is how others perceive you. Introverts are often mistaken for shy or anxious people, as you can imagine, and it happens primarily with strangers. Look at how you are seen by those who know you. If they can observe that you are usually quiet, somewhat reserved, and not eager to share the more intimate corners of your mind, you are probably an introvert.

Shyness

It can be argued that shyness has a lot more in common with social anxiety than introversion does. Of course, shyness is a concept that's a bit difficult to define. It's not a disorder or any sort of diagnosed illness and is much more informal and colloquial of an idea, so to speak. Different people might describe different traits as shyness. Just having one bad day where you don't feel particularly sociable can lead some folks to consider you as shy, even though you're usually not withdrawn at all.

Perhaps the most accurate definition of shyness would be to go back to the fear of judgment that happens with social anxiety as well. Some would describe shyness as a low-intensity or early-stage social anxiety. While they're not the same thing, social anxiety does indeed often look like shyness multiplied by ten. As such, shyness also often stems from simpler issues like low confidence, a poor self-image, and self-conscious attitudes.

However, the thing about shyness and introversion is that the latter can sometimes be forcibly turned into the former, so to speak. As natural and normal as introversion is, it's no secret that our society favors extroverts. It's certainly not some grand conspiracy to oppress introverts, of course, but that's just the way it is. Humans are social creatures, as we discussed, and our economy, society, and civilization itself all depend on the communication of all sorts. As such, we have naturally ended up with a society where extroverts will thrive.

The reason this is relevant is that regular, extroverted folks will sometimes misinterpret introversion for shyness or perceive it as anti-social, which can lead to introverts being ostracized and alienated. This is because they might feel that the way they are is undesirable and unwelcome, ingraining in them a belief that there is something fundamentally wrong with them. Of course, being alienated and shunned is devastating for any person's self-image, and, over time, that's how a healthy introvert might turn into a person suffering from SAD or a considerable level of shyness.

As Jonathan Rauch explained in a rather famous article in the Atlantic in the early 2000s, extroverts find it very difficult to understand the very idea of introversion. They can't relate to it, and this often leads to the misconceptions that we mentioned. Because of all this, introverts can even be labeled as arrogant, stuck-up, and much else.

Another core difference between introversion and shyness is that, unlike introversion, what we call shyness is often a response, not an inherent trait. Apart from just being shy, people can also get shy, in a situation that is. When you feel discomfort in a social situation, and that unpleasant feeling of being judged comes over you, you will usually end up being "shy."

As you can see, shyness can also be viewed and defined as a symptom of social anxiety disorder. But of course, it's not always like that, especially not in colloquial terms and everyday situations. Regular people generally consider shyness to be a trait, and there is a fine balance that some people manage to create between their ability to socialize and their reserved nature. In fact, as you probably know, shyness is sometimes even seen as a virtue or at least as something likable or cute.

This is why shyness is perhaps the murkiest of all these concepts and the most difficult one to define. It's a word that we use so frequently that it's difficult to ascribe a scientific meaning and definition to it. As such, it's best to focus on the differences between introversion and social anxiety above all while considering shyness as a potential symptom of SAD.

One of the many attempts to define shyness was offered by experts in child behavior and personality psychology, Louis A. Schmidt and Arnold H. Buss. They have explained that sociability, as the opposite of shyness, represents a motivation to be with others. Shyness, on the other hand, refers to tension and discomfort among people, and usually certain behaviors in reaction to that discomfort.

Chapter Three: Anxiety vs. Worry vs. Fear

Anxiety has a lot in common with worry and especially with fear, but they're not all one and the same as far as psychology and psychiatry are concerned. This is the chapter where we will go into more detail on what anxiety, in general, really is and how it relates to some common psychological turmoil that we all experience at some point. In the previous chapter, we looked at personality traits that can resemble social anxiety while, in this one, we will focus on mental processes that every healthy human will experience at some point.

Indeed, there is hardly anything more natural and human than worrying or being fearful. Worrying means we care, and it can be very important, especially when it comes to our loved ones. Worrying can also give us signals and warnings as to potentially negative outcomes of certain choices or situations. Furthermore, fear is an indispensable part of our survival mechanism, and it has been as such for as long as we have walked the Earth.

The Shades and Structure of Anxiety

On top of what we have already discussed about the nature of social anxiety and its definition, it's also worth mentioning that social anxiety certainly exists on a spectrum and can be broken down into components. We already discussed early on how symptoms of social anxiety can be categorized, but there is also a three-part view of the structure of anxiety, which some experts will use.

Simply put, the three central components of your anxiety are the emotional, physiological, and cognitive components. The emotional component comprises the things you feel, such as fear or that sinking feeling of dread before a social engagement, for example. The physiological component just includes all those physical symptoms we discussed earlier. The cognitive component is where things get interesting, and this is also where worry falls in. This component is all about the thoughts you have, which are related to your anxiety.

Whenever you think about how you can't do something or about the many potential scenarios where you are embarrassed and humiliated, that's the cognitive component to your anxiety. As you can see, all of this will often entail worrying, and that's how worry comes into play when you're feeling anxious, especially before a social interaction takes place.

We also mentioned that social anxiety disorder exists on a certain spectrum. This is because, as we mentioned, a degree of anxiety happens naturally to most people at some point. The thing about normal anxiety, social or otherwise, is that it won't interfere in your daily life. This is because it happens rarely and because its symptoms are milder than with actual social anxiety disorder. When it occurs in this healthy, natural way, anxiety can even be good. In a social situation, that tiny amount of anxiety can make you more alert, focused, and lively, which some people will interpret positively.

As you start moving away from that side of the spectrum, you approach the levels of anxiety that can cause discomfort and make social situations undesirable for you. Further toward the other end, disorder territory begins when your anxiety hinders your performance in social and other situations and simply impairs you in anything from important tasks to daily life. In other words, it is natural sometimes to worry, but the moment you get to a situation where you would rather just stay home than face the music is when you should know that you probably have social anxiety.

There is also a certain gray area between natural anxiety and full-on impairment. This is where you might get symptoms of an anxiety disorder to a point where you experience regular discomfort. Nonetheless, you will probably find yourself limiting your social interactions and being less assertive, even though you are at least leaving your home. This level of social anxiety can be damaging for you in the long term as it can make you more reserved and unwilling to go the extra mile at work, for instance. Furthermore, being close to diagnosable social anxiety usually means the problem will get worse over time if you leave it unchecked.

Social anxiety can also come accompanied by panic attacks, which are sometimes similar but definitely not the same as anxiety attacks. Panic attacks are characterized by strong physical symptoms or at least a perception of such symptoms. Panic attacks are usually sudden and are triggered due to certain phobias, such as social phobia, in your case. One common physical symptom is an erratic heart rate and difficulties with breathing. Panic attacks won't kill you or give you an actual heart attack, but they can make you feel like it, which makes them scary.

There can be certain continuity between your anxiety and a panic attack because a panic attack can come as a sort of culmination of your anxiety. If you're being stressed out by a prolonged and highly unpleasant social situation, you might get to an overload where your mind just can't take it anymore and moves on to a whole new level of the fear response. Such a thing will never happen because of plain old worry. Panic attacks are very often indicative of an underlying anxiety problem and are always a sign of stress overload. All in all, even though it's a diagnosed mental disorder, social anxiety can sometimes be difficult to define, and it can involve a lot of gray areas.

Anxiety and Worry

Like fear, stress, or shyness, worry has something of a special relationship with anxiety while not being synonymous with it. As you well know, worry is an integral part of the symptoms of social anxiety, although it is sometimes confused with the disorder. It is natural and, in fact, characteristic of humans to engage in planning, as being able to make plans has been one of the decisive factors in getting us to where we are as a species.

Of course, to plan is to think ahead, consider different outcomes, and visualize scenarios. This will inevitably sometimes lead to worry, especially when the odds are objectively stacked against you, for instance. Worry is also normal if you're scheduled for an important job interview or any other social engagement that can directly impact the subsequent course of your life. Simply put, we worry often, and we often have good reasons to do so. Not only that, but worrying is sometimes the thing that keeps us going and helps us make the right decisions.

Still, that doesn't change the fact that worry also plays a prominent role in social anxiety. You now know how worry and anxiety relate to each other, but it's still possible to confuse the two since, as we mentioned, there's the natural worry that everyone experiences, and then there's the kind of worry that comes with outbreaks of anxiety.

One of the most important and immediately obvious differences between worry and anxiety, social or otherwise, is the physical nature of anxiety. Indeed, worry doesn't manifest physically and is instead limited to the confines of your mind. As such, if you have troubling thoughts about something that might happen, even if they get a bit uncontrollable, take note of whether you are experiencing the physical symptoms that we have discussed.

Furthermore, when social anxiety is involved, your worries will get extremely persistent, frequent, and often disproportionate or excessive. It's usually not good to compare yourself to others, but if you worry about going to the store with the same intensity as your friends or family members worry about a potentially life-changing job interview, then you have definitely moved past regular worry.

As we mentioned earlier, one of the key differences between anxiety and worry is that worry is all about what's going on in your thoughts while anxiety gets physical. Since both scenarios involve lots of thinking, though, it's also worth pointing out that worry is usually more specific than anxiety. What that means is that worry tends to focus on a very specific, real issue, whether it's small or big. You can be worried about being late to an appointment, but if you're also troubled by commuting or are obsessing over what might happen once you get to the appointment, then you are anxious. Anxiety is more general and can often get murky when it comes to its sources.

Another important difference is that worry can be productive, at least in the sense that it will often lead you to think of solutions to a problem. It's only natural that when you are worried about a specific issue, your mind will start to think of solutions to that problem. With anxiety, though, no solutions are found because the problem itself is not clear. Anxiety is unproductive and leaves you with no ideas as to how to get through a certain situation. It just gives you stress and fear.

Indeed, just focusing on your actual concerns and analyzing them as objectively as you can give you a better idea of whether you're anxious or just worrying. Next time you get to feeling worried or anxious, you should take a moment to consider what's bothering you. If you are concerned about going to work because you're up for a review, then you are worrying about a specific thing. If, on the other hand, you don't feel like going to work simply because you're afraid you might mess something up or get embarrassed in some way, this would be anxiety.

Worries are also easier to control than anxiety. This is in part because of what we just discussed about worry being more firmly rooted in reality. It's thus easier to get to the underlying problem and solve it, whereas anxiety is something you must struggle against on a much deeper level. Therefore, it is no surprise that worry also tends to be much more temporary than anxiety, which can linger, evolve, and get even more complex and unreasonable. In the simplest possible terms, worry is normal; anxiety is not.

Anxiety and Fear

The relationship between fear and anxiety is very similar to that of anxiety and worry. Just like worry, fear is natural, normal, and even helpful, so it differs from anxiety even though it is one of its common symptoms. Fear is even more specific and focused than worry. Whereas your anxiety is diffuse, your fear response is usually brought on by something very real and immediate – something that's easily identified. Unlike with the general feeling of dread that torments you in seemingly normal social situations, your fear is what alerts you to danger, lets you know when to act, and would keep you alive in the wilderness.

Fear can have many of the same symptoms as anxiety, particularly physical symptoms. It can make you sweat or tremble, and it can hike up your heart rate, but the difference is that the threat is real, while, with anxiety, it is imagined or blown completely out of proportion in your mind. Both fear and anxiety can cause each other or make each other worse as well.

Once again, unlike anxiety, fear is something that isn't chronic, and it doesn't have the potential to ruin your life. It will come and go, and as unpleasant as it might be, it will go away when it's no longer needed or justified. In social situations, fear can be justified in many instances, especially when strangers are involved. It's natural to respond with at least a small amount of fear if you're approached by someone in a dark alleyway. Your mind is analyzing the setting, and it seems quite a few real possibilities of danger, so it warns you about that. On the other hand, if you react to interaction in the same way when you are going to the bank, for instance, then you most likely have social anxiety instead of any fear of a real threat.

In a way, fear is anxiety, and anxiety is fear. This is because they are so similar in nature, while only their root cause is different. It is also that difference in causes that make anxiety a persistent, nagging feeling while fear is very temporary. Anxiety persists because it is caused by such vague and abstract threats that only exist in the projected and imagined scenario that has emerged in your mind. It's difficult to solve a problem that you can't really see or even describe to someone else, so anxiety remains, and it follows you around.

After a while, you can get to a point where your anxiety has caused enough tangible damage to your life for you to start fearing the anxiety itself. And why wouldn't you? If it has damaged your career, caused you embarrassment, and devastated your social life, your social anxiety is a threat to you – a very real and objective one at that. It is certainly a strange blend of real and abstract since the anxiety itself is just in your mind, but it's a very real vicious cycle that many sufferers of SAD end up in.

As you can see, fear, worry, and shyness all have connections and relationships with social anxiety disorder, and why they are not synonymous, they play prominent parts. All three of these things can occur naturally, but when social anxiety is at play, all three can become persistent and exhausting. As you will learn through this book, this whole problem can be approached from both ends. Namely, some folks have successfully beaten their social anxiety disorders by attacking their fears and worries head-on. On the other hand, some prefer to address the disorder through therapy and other such approaches that go straight to the disease.

In either case, the result will be the same if you are successful. The chronic and irrational aspect of these feelings is what you must remove from your life. You will still get to feel fear and worry, of course, and you might even get shy at times, but you will no longer be at the whim of your unpredictable and ever-present anxiety. In a way, the goal is not just to interact and socialize like a regular person, but also to fear and to worry like a regular, healthy person.

Chapter Four: Ten Common Fears Introverts Have

As we already discussed, introversion is something that people often confuse with social anxiety. Regardless, social anxiety is indeed often part of an introvert's life, and so the two do correlate. Because of this, we can understand social anxiety better if we also get a better understanding of the introverted mind. In this chapter, we will go over some of the situations and experiences that introverts might fear or prefer to avoid, especially if they have social anxiety. This should help you get an even better understanding of the differences between anxiety and introversion but also how they can work together at times.

This list should also help you categorize some of your experiences and reactions to certain situations. You will thus be better equipped to identify whether you're struggling with anxiety or are just introverted. For each of these situations or environments, we will also consider how a socially anxious individual might react to them as opposed to someone who is merely an introvert.

Small Talk

Like most things we'll discuss in this chapter, small talk is something that comes completely naturally to folks who have no problems with social interaction. It's something that's meant to pass the time, allow us to analyze the other person, or just entertain us. Introverts are usually not fans of small talk and meaningless chit-chat, in general, but that's not always because they fear it.

When social anxiety is at play, however, small talk becomes scary because, instead of being a frivolous pastime, it provides ample opportunity to feel judged and scrutinized. A socially anxious person will spend every second of that small talk obsessing over how they look or sound and constantly fretting over what the other person might be thinking about them. Even when it's obvious that the conversational partner is not judgmental or noticing anything strange about us, the mind that's stricken with social anxiety will be clouded by irrational fear.

In fact, small talk might be one of the worst and most stressful forms of conversation that a socially anxious person might get into. When a conversation is deep, thoughtful, meaningful, and, most importantly, interesting, it will captivate the mind more easily and direct the thoughts away from that anxious path. You should consider the way you think and act during small talk to see where you fall on the spectrum.

Crowds

This one is something of a no-brainer, but crowds are something that's very difficult for introverts to deal with. Introverts will prefer calmer, quieter settings such as resting at home or sitting around with a select group of close friends. As such, introverts tend to avoid crowds simply because they don't get anything out of the experience. When they are also socially anxious, though, they will see crowds as a scary prospect, not just a hassle.

The fear will be exacerbated if the socially anxious introvert is alone. Think about a scenario such as being alone in a bar or at a party and how it would make you feel or how it has made you feel if you've ever experienced it. Crowded places have a way of making some people feel even more alone than usual, especially if they are introverted. Your social anxiety might also make you feel like everyone is judging you, and this feeling can make people seem inaccessible. When feeling alone or left out in such a setting, the normal course of action is to start up a conversation with someone, but social anxiety makes that incredibly difficult. The sight of others engaging in conversations so effortlessly and having great fun can also make matters worse.

Healthy introverts will sincerely and wholeheartedly prefer to sit at home by the fireplace and read a book, with that being the reason they don't go to parties. Socially anxious folks, on the other hand, will not go because of their fears, even though they might yearn for the experience.

Meeting New People

As we just mentioned, social anxiety makes it incredibly difficult to approach people and start conversations, which makes meeting new people a chore. The thing about introverts, even socially anxious ones, is that they might already have a couple of close friends, especially if they are childhood friends, and still struggle to meet new people. Because of this, just because you have some friends doesn't mean that you're not socially anxious or introverted.

Meeting new people is difficult for socially anxious people both as a prospect and as a reality when it happens. This means that SAD will make you want to avoid situations where you know you might get to meet someone new. You might feel deep down like you have a desire to meet new people, but your fear of judgment and embarrassment will often be stronger than that desire.

Something that healthy introverts should have no problem with is being approached by a stranger and engaging in conversation with them. When you have social anxiety, interaction is stressful even when the other person initiates contact and breaks the ice. You might begin feeling the symptoms and then start to worry about the person noticing there's something wrong with you, and things can spiral out of control in no time.

Giving a Speech

Giving a speech is a nightmare for many people, and it can be stressful even for extroverts, depending on the situation and how important the speech is. Introverts don't enjoy being the center of attention at gatherings, and they certainly prefer to stick to the sidelines while others do the public speaking. For socially anxious folks, on the other hand, giving a speech is a scenario that probably most closely resembles hell.

It's unfortunate that a lot of regular people don't really have much understanding of introverts, much less those with social anxiety. In settings like weddings or other familial gatherings, introverts are sometimes pushed by others into situations where they must speak. The thing is, though, that most people aren't gifted speakers, and they will generally try to avoid that role by default, so it doesn't necessarily imply that social anxiety is at play.

Regular folks will be able to improvise, though, and they won't find the possibility of embarrassment as terrifying as socially anxious people will. As such, if you're merely reluctant but still don't start feeling nauseous, dizzy, or panicked, it's just your introversion.

Public Transport and Elevators

Public transport is a double-edged sword when it comes to social anxiety. It's difficult to determine which is worse: when the train or bus is absolutely packed with strangers or when there's just you and one or two other people, increasing the chances of you drawing their attention.

Public transportation can get really crowded, so it's only natural to be annoyed when your personal space is being invaded and when you're physically uncomfortable. Regular introverts will deal with these conditions by shutting the world off via headphones and music or by reading a book. Social anxiety can make even that difficult, though, as the feeling of being watched or judged can sometimes be intense enough to break through your attempts at distraction.

Elevators are another problem area when you have social anxiety. The upside is that the elevator ride is usually over very quickly, but the confined space of the elevator can make for some rather awkward moments when you find yourselves in there with only one other person. Again, a regular introvert will be able to just keep to themselves for a few seconds and go about their business; however, with social anxiety, that short elevator ride can be incredibly stressful and mentally exhausting.

Open-Plan Offices

Introverts tend to feel the most comfortable on jobs where they get to work alone for extended periods or are at least given an office of their own where they can retreat. Open-plan offices are severely restricting when it comes to privacy, so this can be a very exhausting environment for an introvert, especially when there's also social anxiety to contend with.

However, the human brain's ability to adapt to a routine is quite impressive! If a routine is solid and predictable enough, even a socially anxious person can get used to an environment such as this. If there are always the same people around, with the same conditions and the same sort of work and interaction, you might get used to it after a while and function normally while at work. As soon as you find yourself in a new situation, or there is a sudden change; however, your anxiety might kick right back in.

Because of this, you shouldn't be confused if you find yourself talking to your coworkers and working with them without a problem, but then fail to interact with people at a bar or some other such place. What's more, introverts can get incredibly communicative and sociable once they get used to a circle of people, to a point where, when observed from the side, they seem extroverted.

Phone Calls

Outbreaks of social anxiety are not exclusive to face-to-face interactions. Making phone calls is something that most introverts don't enjoy, except when it's to someone they are completely comfortable with. Social anxiety makes phone calls difficult on a whole new level, though, especially when the call is important or involves a stranger.

Regular folks can go on and on over the phone while doing other things around the house or even while working. With social anxiety, though, your mind will be unable to focus on anything other than the phone call, and you will either sit frozen in place or pace around the room nervously the entire time. Physical symptoms of anxiety and all the discomfort that they bring might then ensue. You might start having shortness of breath, and your voice might begin to shake.

As usual, when those symptoms happen, there will be a high possibility of further fears over the other person noticing there's something wrong, further worsening the anxiety. For socially anxious folks, the only advantage of phone calls is that they can usually be promptly cut off. Other than that, for many sufferers of SAD, phone calls are just as stressful as personal interactions. Furthermore, telephonophobia is a phobia that exists, and it's exactly what you would imagine. The fear of making phone calls and the fear of social interaction can essentially make phone calls the scariest form of interaction for some introverts.

Surprises

Surprises - particularly those that entail social situations and interactions - are a great enemy of many introverts, especially socially anxious ones. Things that break routines and cause upsets that can lead to unexpected situations and unexpected people can be dreadful. These surprises can entail big changes in the work environment, for instance, in which case they are there to stay, but they can also come in the form of more trivial situations like surprise parties.

As you can imagine, a sudden and unexpected social situation is not something that introverts are known to enjoy, much less when they struggle with social anxiety. If you've ever been thrown a surprise party or experienced something similar, you should know how it made you feel. Extroverts would immediately know how to act, and they would probably be happy to receive such attention, but introversion and social anxiety can lead to a panicked response.

Of course, the main problem with these situations is in the very center of attention for everyone in the room. As usual, that kind of spotlight is a socially anxious person's greatest fear. Still, surprise parties might have a different effect in some instances. For some people, social anxiety is at its worst when a social situation is anticipated, and when they have plenty of time to obsess over it and think of a million negative scenarios. A surprise party might occupy your mind immediately and not give you any time to think, which can be a good thing with social anxiety.

Scrutiny

Any kind of scrutiny can be difficult for folks with social anxiety, especially in public. Therefore, things like job interviews are so difficult for introverted folks. It's not just a question of fearing the scrutiny itself, either. You might end up being afraid of showing symptoms of your anxiety while being scrutinized, even if you're confident in your knowledge, skill, or competence.

For instance, people with social anxiety are often afraid to write in front of others. They are afraid that their hand will start to shake, and that the other person will notice it. It's one of those situations where anxiety and the fear of that anxiety feed into each other and form a stressful cycle. There are countless other similar examples, some of which you have likely experienced at some point. Therefore, socially anxious people can fail where they shouldn't.

As an example, they can study for a long time and be well-prepared for a test, but the unbearable discomfort of scrutiny can still make them fail the test. It's why they end up not getting jobs that they are qualified for or a promotion that they more than deserve. It's unfair, and it amounts to nothing short of being robbed of all the good things in life.

Embarrassment

Last (but not least), embarrassment, particularly in public, is something that's very difficult to deal with for introverts - let alone socially anxious ones! As mentioned before, in most cases of social anxiety disorder, the fear of embarrassment is the very core of the condition.

Certainly, everybody can get embarrassed or humiliated, but the difference between regular folks and those with social anxiety is that the former doesn't spend a lot of time thinking about the prospect of embarrassment, whereas the latter does. The potential to get embarrassed is usually the first thing to pop into the mind of a socially anxious person when they consider a possible social situation they might get into. The fear is the most decisive factor that makes you avoid social situations or gives you second thoughts.

People who are only introverted might not handle embarrassment well, but they won't have the same obsession with that risk prior to the situation. Furthermore, social anxiety can make you feel embarrassed even though there really isn't anything to be embarrassed about. This is especially true when there's low self-esteem at play, as it can make you much more likely to feel embarrassed or humiliated.

That's how and why those situations and settings affect introverts or introverts with social anxiety. It's another list that can function as a checklist of symptoms and signs for you to use to get better acquainted with your case.

Chapter Five: How Psychological Triggers Work

Of course, social anxiety doesn't just come up out of nowhere. We already mentioned a thing or two about the cause of the disorder itself, but now we will look at what goes on in your brain when any individual anxiety attack occurs. This chapter is all about understanding your own mind better in addition to getting to know more about what social anxiety is and how it works.

We also listed several potentially triggering situations and how introverts and socially anxious folks might react to them. These situations can be viewed as psychological triggers that lead to outbursts of anxiety, but why and how does that happen? What is it that your mind is doing wrong, and how can you begin to fix it? The truth is that your mind and instincts are doing what they were designed to do, but they are doing it at the wrong time and under the wrong circumstances.

Something else we'll look at is the concept of psychological triggers in relation to things like post-traumatic stress. This can be another source of social and any other kind of anxiety, so it's another important topic to discuss in that it will help you understand anxiety even better.

The Inner-Workings of Anxiety

As we mentioned, your anxiety is a fear response that becomes chronic and revolves around mostly abstract objects of fear. You can view your anxiety as a malfunction of your natural survival mechanisms that are otherwise useful and necessary. It's as if you had an important and sophisticated alarm system in your home, which, unfortunately, goes off all the time, ringing and blaring for no good reason at all, driving you nuts.

When it works like it's meant to, your flight-or-fight response is indeed supposed to stress you out, but that's just for a little while and because it's meant to give you a temporary boost to help you escape or fight the threat. This is something that virtually all animals have in some form of another. You might be inclined to think that the malfunctions of this system, like anxiety, are uniquely human, but that's not true. Animals can be traumatized, for instance, causing them to remember the trauma and experience severe anxiety whenever they are reminded of it.

Furthermore, take the example of a dog that was too sheltered and not properly exposed to the world like a puppy. Such dogs will often grow up to be anxious and afraid in all unfamiliar environments and situations. We're not much different at all with both examples. Our anxieties, social or otherwise, can often be tied to past trauma that's brought back every time the internalized stressful memory gets triggered, as we'll discuss in a bit more detail soon. On top of that, the more we isolate ourselves from the world, the worse our insecurities and anxieties will get. Children who have trouble socializing or are overly sheltered, for instance, will often develop social anxiety or a range of other behavioral issues. Of course, as you know by now, these things are only some of the potential causes of anxiety. The difficulty of identifying the real, underlying cause is really one of the characteristics of anxiety, to begin with.

We do, however, have a rather detailed understanding of the inner workings of anxiety and of the process involved. As usual, your brain acts first, and then the body follows. Like most things, anxiety and fear have specific parts of the brain that are responsible for regulating them. We know this thanks to brain imaging technology and our understanding of neurochemicals and what they do. To put things simply, the two parts of your brain that are usually at the epicenter of almost all anxiety disorders are the amygdala and the hippocampus.

These parts of your brain have roles that are very important and extend well beyond just your simple fear responses. Your amygdala, located deep in your brain, is like an intersection or hub for communications. The parts of your brain that register and process sensory signals and the parts that make sense of those signals use the amygdala to communicate with each other. Being at such a junction, the amygdala is in the position to detect those signals that can be interpreted as threatening.

As such, the amygdala can put your brain on alert and lead to a fear response when needed. Your amygdala can also store memories that are emotional in nature, such as attachments or associations between certain things you have experienced. Therefore, the amygdala is believed to play a role in all sorts of fear-related things, including anxiety disorders and phobias.

On the other hand, the hippocampus deals specifically with memorizing and internalizing events and experiences where you were threatened or felt as such. The role of the hippocampus in things like flashbacks, trauma, post-traumatic stress, and similar problems is still being studied. Researchers have hitherto managed to confirm that the hippocampus in people who were exposed to abuse as children or have participated in a war is smaller. It's not the case 100% of the time, but there is a strong correlation, as outlined by the National Institute of Mental Health.

Without going into too much scientific detail, something else you should keep in mind is the role of neurochemicals in the process behind your anxiety. When your mind and body enter their flight-or-fight mode, your brain will ramp up the production of organic chemicals like norepinephrine and hormones like cortisol. Cortisol is an especially famous one, and it is commonly referred to as the stress hormone.

Both substances are completely natural and normal, as their role is to give you important boosts in potentially life-threatening situations. Their purpose is to make you alert, quick, and overall stimulated. This is what leads to all those physiological symptoms that we have discussed, like a heightened heart rate and erratic breathing. In this state, your body and mind will disregard or outright shut down many other processes so that they can both focus on one simple task, which is to keep you alive.

In your case, your mind has become convinced that it is the threat of humiliation and embarrassment that is life-threatening, so it acts accordingly. Both your mind and body are doing what they are supposed to do, but they are doing it for the wrong reason, and that's the core of the problem. That is how anxiety emerges and how it works. The cause is one thing, but there are also triggers, such as those we have discussed in the previous chapter. There are also triggers that can be more personal and internalized, as opposed to completely external.

Psychological Triggers

Psychological triggers are something that can often be the thing that sets an individual's anxiety in motion. The triggers themselves usually have an underlying cause, such as trauma, so they can't really be the cause of social anxiety in their own right. They can, however, provide the spark that provokes an anxious response, which, in turn, can lead to an exacerbated anxiety brought on by the fear of these triggers.

A psychological trigger can come in many forms, including smells, sights, sounds, or other things that can trigger a traumatic response. Therefore, triggers are usually associated with things like post-traumatic stress disorder, or PTSD. These triggers are reminders, and they bring to the surface and internalized memory and fear of a trauma that has transpired in the past. Such reminders of traumatic experiences usually lead to anxiety, panic attacks, or at least an intense sense of dread. In more extreme cases, the sufferer can also experience flashbacks.

These vivid outbursts of involuntary and accurate remembering can feel like the person is reliving the traumatic event all over again. Flashbacks can lead to a complete albeit temporary dissociation from the environment and from the current reality. People who experience flashbacks can "lose" time or become utterly disoriented for a while. As such, the anxiety can be just one of the symptoms, and when such responses occur in social situations, traumatized people can be mistaken for just being socially anxious when, in fact, the problem is even deeper.

These triggers can include the simplest, most innocuous of things, if these things can - in some way - bring up past trauma. Sometimes, the response can come about as a result of too much stress as well, in which case the trigger isn't even external. As you can probably imagine, a simple example of one of these triggers can be a smell that the sufferer has smelled during the traumatic event. A war veteran, for instance, can be triggered by the smell of gunpowder. There can really be a million different triggers in a million different personal stories of trauma.

We still don't know everything about how and why our minds internalize and respond to these triggers the way they do. Some believe that it once again all goes back to our fight or flight response in situations perceived to be threatening. The most bewildering thing about trauma, triggers, and all these other things is that different people can be affected differently by the same things. Not everyone who was abused as a child will carry the trauma, some people come back from war mostly unchanged, and some, even though they are traumatized, won't necessarily be triggered and anxious.

We mentioned earlier that your mind and body would disregard various processes that aren't essential for survival when a flight-or-fight situation arises. One of these processes is the formation of your short-term memories. Herein lays one of the theories about how psychological triggers work. Namely, it's possible that your brain can take an ongoing traumatic experience and store it in the wrong file cabinet, so to speak.

Instead of putting this event into the category of past events that become regular memories, like the time you went to the beach, your brain can categorize the event as an ongoing threat. As such, every reminder (trigger) will bring that experience back to the surface, even years down the road, and your brain will be tricked into thinking that it's happening again. Your mind and body will then enter flight-or-fight mode again, and you will shut down and become unable to control your anxiety or outright panic.

You can imagine how this plays out in the context of social anxiety. If a past trauma revolves around public humiliation, bullying, or something similar, it's not difficult to see how the most public, social situations could act as a trigger.

Something else that experts have been looking at is the sensory component in triggers. Things like sights, sounds, smells, and tastes are some of the strongest building blocks for memories. As such, the most intense and vivid memories are often those that include sensory stimuli, especially smell and taste. Such memories are also the easiest to remember, so a trigger that involves these senses can be incredibly powerful.

If you've ever experienced the onset of memories that can happen when you taste a certain dish or smell something, then you have seen this mechanism at work. Your brain is simply wired to take special note of that sensory information, and that comes into play during regular and traumatic events alike.

Another thing about these sensory triggers is that they can work alone, regardless of context. You can find yourself in a situation that's completely different than the one where the traumatic event took place, but if you sense the triggering smell, for instance, it will be enough to cause a reaction.

As such, these sensory triggers can also be rather *stealthy*. You might get anxious or otherwise emotional even before you realize what's happening and why, and you might not even notice the smell or connect it to what you are feeling. Your brain notices these things, though, and unless you know how to listen, it can be difficult to get to the root of the problem.

What's particularly tricky about all this is that such triggers can lead to episodes that can be misinterpreted as social anxiety. For instance, a sensory trigger of past trauma can occur while you are in a social situation, leading to an outbreak of anxiety or a panic attack even if the trauma has nothing to do with social situations. Interacting with people in such a state is going to be difficult, of course, so it might come across as social anxiety.

The ways in which you can deal with these triggers are as variable as the triggers and their causes. If your triggers indeed have to do with socializing or if you harbor past traumas associated with social situations, then the methods we will discuss throughout the rest of this book can help you. However, as we just discussed, psychological triggers can be tied to many experiences that don't have to do with socializing. In those cases, it might be a good idea to seek professional help, especially if you are having difficulties identifying the source of these triggers in the first place.

You should especially talk to a professional if you have reason to believe that you might be suffering from PTSD; it is very serious condition that can lead to a whole range of complications, including a complete breakdown - or even death. Healing from PTSD can be a long and painful journey that will require not just the help of professionals, but also that of your loved ones.

That's what psychological triggers are and how they work, particularly in the context of trauma, stress, and anxiety. It's not something that anybody should have to live with, and it's certainly not a problem that should be avoided or catered to. If certain things trigger anxious or panic reactions from you, then you should address the problem instead of just avoiding the trigger. Of course, if the reactions are extreme, then full and abrupt exposure is not the way to go, but gradual exposure and conditioning will usually be parts of the treatment in such cases.

Chapter Six: Negative Thoughts – Identify and Break Out of Them

As you have undoubtedly realized by now, social anxiety is largely based on a cycle of negative thoughts that are usually irrational and do little more than getting your mind racing and your thoughts clouded. Although some of the worries that trouble folks with SAD are universal, these negative thoughts usually vary from one individual to the next. An important step toward beating your social anxiety will be to identify your negative thoughts and your mental patterns that lead to a downward spiral of anxiety. You will then have to learn how to break free from these thoughts and, better yet, replace them with positive ones.

We've already briefly mentioned the importance of thinking positively, but, in this chapter, we will go into more detail on how exactly you can categorize the contents of your mind and clean up troubling thoughts. Rewiring your brain in this way can entail a lot of work, and it tends to be more difficult than many people anticipate, but every person who isn't severely mentally ill has the capacity to put a leash on their thoughts and get back in the driver's seat, *and you do, too.*

Understanding and Identifying Negative Thought Patterns

Negative thoughts can be strangely appealing to a mind that's used to them. What's more, when you indulge in certain negative thoughts for a while, they can easily snowball, getting worse over time. Because our brains naturally respond to patterns, they sometimes have a strange way of getting tangled up in patterns of negative thinking. This is how your thoughts can spiral uncontrollably and lead to a complete breakdown of reason during an anxious episode.

You may become so accustomed to these thoughts that you arrive at a place where you don't even know that the thoughts you are having are negative and detrimental for you. Therefore, the first step is to learn how to *identify negative thoughts and find the patterns in your thinking* that need to be dealt with.

After a while of living with low self-esteem and constantly delving into negative thinking, you will likely also develop automatic negative thoughts. These are thoughts that more closely resemble a sort of self-deprecating reflex that occurs every time you think of a potential social situation. For instance, if, upon being invited to go to a party, the first thing that come to mind is that you will be made fun of or that you will just embarrass yourself, then you are trapped in a cycle of automatic negative thoughts. This is usually what comes of prolonged social anxiety that's left unchecked.

This sort of thinking can quickly become routine as your mind loves nothing more than to recognize patterns and get comfortable in a routine. The degree to which your thoughts can influence and shape your feelings and life, in general, is underestimated. That goes for both conscious thoughts and those that are more involuntary and automatic.

Being that they are so deeply ingrained and involuntary, your automatic thoughts can be rather elusive, so identifying them might take some work. One of the ways to do this is to write down as many of your thoughts as you can - especially those that have to do with your self-image and opinion of yourself. The contents of our minds tend to look a whole lot different when we put them down on paper; on paper, we can take a more objective look and inspect that information with more impartiality.

You should try and do this on the fly, writing the thoughts down precisely when they happen instead of sitting down in the afternoon and trying to remember the thoughts. You can use your phone or a small notebook for this purpose and just write down what comes to mind in simple notes. As you write, you are likely to get even more thoughts going in your head, and because you will be writing, all of them will appear clearer. Don't focus too much on judging these thoughts or thinking about them. It's usually even better if you simply write them down and then look at the notes later.

You might be surprised to learn just how much negativity there is in your thoughts and how quickly you are to indulge them. With social anxiety, your mind will get flooded by negative thoughts in normal social situations, not just situations where you get embarrassed or experience some sort of failure. This habit of quickly jumping into a whirl of negativity is referred to as "negativity bias" by many neuroscientists and psychologists.

And that's precisely what it is – you simply have a bias toward the negative side of things, and that's what needs changing or at least controlling. The thing about your negativity bias is that it's natural to a degree, once again going back to survival instincts from our cave-dwelling days. The assumption of the worst-case scenario was useful and lifesaving for our ancestors in the wild, but these days, it can be a nuisance. Of course, the real problems begin when the negativity bias goes into the extreme.

This whole process was described in detail by Rick Hanson, a neuroscientist, and author of <u>Buddha's Brain</u>. In this book, Hanson describes the proclivity of your mind to focus on the negative while disregarding the positive experiences. When you have even more negative experiences than the regular person, which is all but guaranteed with social anxiety, your brain will eventually get outright obsessive with its focus on the negative side of everything.

Common Negative Thinking Patterns

The patterns and cycles of intensely negative thinking can vary a lot from one person to the next, but some patterns are universal and are experienced by most anxious people at some point. You are likely to identify with most if not all of these if you have social anxiety. Even without anxiety, though, many people can still fall into these patterns at least for a short while at some point in their lives.

One example of a negative thinking pattern is what can be referred to as cynical hostility. This one is especially characteristic of social anxiety and even plain introversion. As you might have gathered from the term itself, this is an attitude of deep distrust and hostility, whether internal or expressed, toward other people. This tends to happen when a person spends enough time with a disdain for social interaction or has accumulated enough negative experiences.

Of course, the troublesome part is that these negative experiences could have transpired because of the person's social anxiety. This means that the negative experience might not have been the fault of other people or, in some cases, even real. Social anxiety can certainly make you anxious and turn an interaction into an unpleasant memory even if nothing particularly problematic happens. Just the feeling of anxiety can be enough to create a strong distaste for people, even when the interaction transpires objectively well.

Cynical hostility will make you see the worst in people and always assume that they are doing or planning to do something against you. It is characteristic of hostile cynics to assume that the other person is trying to cheat or lie in some way, and the assumption that the cynic is being judged is also omnipresent. In severe cases, folks can start to project this even on their loved ones and the people they've been close with for years.

This can ruin relationships and lead to all sorts of upheaval and emotional turmoil in your life. Not to mention, some research suggests that there is a correlation between cynical hostility and heart problems later in life. Perhaps the weight of constantly keeping your guard up and always worrying about who is out to get you can wear you out after a couple of decades.

Negative rumination is another big one, especially when you consider the obsessiveness of anxiety. Negative rumination is the psychological and mental equivalent of a hamster wheel or a car stuck in the mud. It exerts a lot of energy and wears you out, but it ultimately gets you nowhere. This pattern is introspection and self-reflection taken to the extreme, particularly the negative extreme.

It occurs when you routinely get fixated on the negative or perceived negative aspects of yourself, reflecting on them to excessive lengths and very frequently, repeatedly. It's also possible to negatively ruminate outward as well, such as when you obsess over negative scenarios and outcomes of in situations that haven't even happened. The same can apply for past events that have left you feeling embarrassed. Negative rumination is when you can't stop thinking about what you did wrong or what you could have done better, to the point of driving yourself almost crazy.

This mental pitfall can exacerbate your anxiety and lead to a lot of other problems like depression, low self-esteem, mood swings, et cetera. Soon enough, you might catch yourself excessively thinking about the very fact that you are feeling anxious and low, which can become an obsession in and of itself.

Next up, you have your plain old overthinking. Overthinking can also take the form of perfectionism, and it usually leads to indecisiveness, reluctance, fear, and anxiety. At the core of the issue lies the false notion that it's possible to avoid all mistakes and remove all risk from the equation, which is, of course, impossible. It is very likely that you are familiar with this thinking pattern.

Whereas regular folks can just seamlessly get into social situations and interact without even thinking about it, people with social anxiety tend to obsess over doing everything right before they get on with it. This just builds up the anxiety and increases your reluctance, often ending with you prefer just to walk away.

These are just some of the negative thinking patterns that you might be familiar with. Perhaps you're so used to them that this is the first time you hear that this sort of thinking is bad for you. Indeed, these mental pitfalls can feel deceptively natural when you have anxiety, but they are really excessing that are making things way more difficult than they should be.

Shifting Your Mindset

Once you have acquainted yourself with the way your mind works and identifies the problematic thoughts that you need to move past, your next step is to shift your thinking and your whole mindset toward the positive. This isn't just about thinking a happy thought when you feel low. The ultimate goal is to permanently change your outlook and shift your mindset in the long term.

Take the patterns we have just discussed, for instance. There are methods you can start implementing right away, which can really alter your outlook and make you see the world in a new light. If you have identified yourself with cynical hostility, you should try to take a mental note of when you are thinking those thoughts and try to find alternatives. In a way, you should try and catch yourself in that pattern and make a conscious effort to replace the thought.

The simplest example is when people give you a compliment. A cynically hostile person will almost always assume there is an ulterior motive at play and that the other person is just flattering them because they want something. Of course, that's usually not the case, and a compliment tends to be just that – a compliment. Try and adopt the same mindset for all sorts of other behaviors that you have interpreted negatively in the past.

Put your judgment and negative assumptions on a leash, and don't let them be the automatic, first response. You can do this by focusing on evidence or the lack thereof. When you get to thinking that the other person is plotting or judging you, ask yourself if you have even a shred of evidence to support that assumption. The chances are good that you will have none. Simply put, you should try and apply the age-old principle of presumed innocence.

Negative rumination is even easier to beat. Since it is a cycle of repetition, all you must do is break that cycle as soon as you notice it's arising. Don't limit yourself just to the thoughts that have to do with your social anxiety or introversion. Whenever you catch yourself ruminating, no matter what it might be about, you should break the cycle. All you must do is give your mind someone else to toy with – ideally something productive and constructive. Creative hobbies are an excellent alternative to sitting and obsessing over thoughts that give you nothing but suffering. It doesn't matter what creative endeavor it is or how unskilled you are; the point is to get your mind busy.

You can also just go walk your dog or go to the store and stock up on groceries or engage in several other menial activities to keep your thoughts at bay. The two things that you should not do, however, are drinking alcohol and overeating just to drown out your mind. These are bad solutions that will almost always do more harm than good.

As for overthinking, the cliché that you should just do it certainly holds true. That's not to say that you shouldn't think about your actions at all, far from it, but the time you spend thinking should be reduced. You should especially cut down on that time when it comes to taking harmless action like talking to people. It's natural to spend some time thinking before you make big life decisions, of course, but thinking of a million (negative) scenarios and outcomes before starting a conversation with a stranger at the park serves virtually no purpose. Besides, the one thing you need to realize and fully internalize is that it's okay to mess up and that even if you get embarrassed, the consequences will be objectively harmless.

What we're talking about is something along the lines of the "notice-shift-rewire" approach. This is a pretty simple strategy to help you rewire your brain and shift its focus toward the positive side of things. This is a well-developed and tested strategy that has been in the works for a long time and has evolved for years.

Basically, the first step is all about noticing that negativity bias in your mind. As we have discussed, it's all about catching yourself in the act. It will probably take some practice to reach this level of awareness, but it's certainly doable. Make sure you use the tips we discussed, such as writing down your thoughts, at least at first.

The "shift" step includes all those changes in thinking that we've mentioned. In general, though, if you are trying to escape from overall negativity as quickly as possible, one recommended approach is to use gratitude. Indeed, just thinking about at least one thing you're grateful for in your life can ground you now and put your obsessive, negative thoughts into a more manageable perspective. You must remember that there is always something. Even if you're bankrupt, you might still have your health. And if you're ill, you probably have parents. If you look hard enough, there will always be something.

The last step that has to do with "rewiring" is the key and the end goal of the whole process. That's what you will essentially be doing – rewiring your brain and changing its habits. All the efforts we have just discussed can be taken up on the fly and integrated into your daily routine. All you must do is remember to bring yourself to the present, be more mindful of your thoughts, and get to work replacing the unwanted ones to get rid of this dead weight. The exercise we will discuss in the next chapter can also be helpful in that regard.

Chapter Seven: How Mindfulness Can Help with Social Anxiety

When it comes to the cognitive side of beating your social anxiety, mindfulness can be an indispensable tool. After all, mindfulness itself is all about cognition and the way you think. In the simplest terms, mindfulness implies being truly present in and engaged with the moment you find yourself in. It is a mental exercise to help you streamline your thoughts, quiet the mental noise, and ultimately put your mind at ease. It's essentially a meditative exercise, but don't let that dissuade you, as it's not a complicated or particularly advanced exercise and can be undertaken by laypersons without a problem.

The value of mindfulness in combating social anxiety is in that it's meant to clear your mind and streamline your thoughts, blocking out the anxiety-inducing mental noise that causes your problem. While you can fight on other fronts to boost your confidence and change your outlook from negative to positive, for instance, mindfulness can be an additional tool to help you rein your mind in for further maintenance. In this chapter, we will take a detailed look at what mindfulness really is and how you can use it to fight social anxiety.

What Is Mindfulness?

In practical terms, mindfulness is a process that is meditative in nature and focuses on shifting your attention in a certain way. That way is toward each present moment that you find yourself in, without worry about the future scenarios or dwelling on past ones. The objective is to help a clouded mind clear up, remove background noise, and focus intently on that which is at hand without judgment. Mindfulness meditation or mindfulness activities can be infused into all sorts of otherwise menial, daily things like breathing, eating, walking, et cetera.

Certainly, being "present" might sound to you as a goal that's rather abstract in nature, but the rewards that come with achieving that state are what you will be after. These can include reduced stress, emotional balance, emotional and mental resilience, clarity of mind, calmness, focus, concentration, and even physical benefits. As you can already see, a lot of those things translate well to your struggle against social anxiety. Imagine being able to block out all those negative thoughts and silence the inner voice that keeps telling you that you are threatened. Therefore, mindfulness is useful in curbing the symptoms of your SAD.

Mindfulness and associated meditative practices can be traced back to Buddhist traditions such as Zen and Vipassana. As such, it has been practiced in Buddhism's native lands in Asia for millennia. The practice started to gain ground and was popularized in the West during the 20th century. Like many other eastern practices such as yoga and other forms of meditation, mindfulness is something that gains more interest every year in the West.

Whether or not this popularity is due to perceived exoticism, meditation undoubtedly helps thousands, if not millions, of people every year. Apart from helping with stress-related issues, mindfulness is also used to alleviate symptoms of depression and even combat drug addiction. Furthermore, mindfulness isn't something that's only practiced by individuals on their own time in the West. In fact, mindfulness has been used in all sorts of environments, ranging from schools to prisons to all sorts of mental institutions.

The time around 1970 was something of a turning point for mindfulness because it started to gain more attention from mainstream psychology after that time. The research done on the subject since then has been rather extensive, although more of it is needed.

The success and usefulness of mindfulness in solving many of the problems we mentioned above have been documented and put to the test by science, with highly positive results. It has been found that mindfulness indeed helps with fighting various mental problems while also helping alleviate some simpler problems like excessive worry. Some research has even suggested that mindfulness is a useful tool in preventing mental health issues. There will have to be more research done in the future, but as things stand now, mindfulness is a proven technique, at least in a sizeable portion of its claims.

Apart from making you more present and focused, mindfulness should also help you get in touch with your emotions and become more aware of yourself as well. Because mindfulness is all about focusing on things without judgment, it won't lead to you ruminating on negative thoughts and making yourself feel worse. The idea is to just be more aware solely as a means of getting to know yourself better.

It's also worth mentioning that the process and the end goal of mindfulness can be achieved through various meditative exercises. Apart from being a practice, mindfulness is also a state of mind, and the roads that will lead there are various. Some people even hire personal trainers and other meditation experts to guide them through meditation exercises that can help achieve mindfulness. Still, you don't have to do that because mindfulness can be incredibly easy to practice.

Mindfulness also won't take up a lot of your time. If you so choose, you will be able to engage in mindfulness meditation for up to 40 or so minutes a day, but you can also spend far less time than that. It will be up to you to decide if you want to take up meditation sessions at home and really allocate that time and effort to turn it into a routine or if you want to do it on the fly. As we mentioned above, mindfulness works well with all sorts of daily activities and can fit seamlessly into your life, which is what makes mindfulness so accessible for all.

Mindfulness for Anxiety

So, how exactly do you go about practicing mindfulness, particularly taking social anxiety into account? It's not much more difficult than it sounds. Namely, it's all about choosing an object of focus and then using that object to ground yourself in the present. This object can be anything from your breathing pattern to a conversation that you might be having with someone.

Because one of the central ideas is non-judgment, the goal is to maintain a certain distance between yourself and the thing you are observing and focusing on, and especially between yourself and your emotional reactions. If you want to take some time out of your day and indulge in a meditation session to achieve mindfulness, you won't need any special equipment or experience. All you will need is some time and a quiet space where you won't be disturbed. You should choose a time of day when your schedule is the lightest and put your phone and other such distractions in another room or turn them off.

If you want to make things easier and more like advanced meditation, you can get yourself a cushion or a soft mat to sit on and assume a meditative pose. One common example is sitting on the ground with your legs crossed, and your hands are resting completely relaxed on your thighs. The important thing is to be relaxed and comfortable physically and to minimize distractions.

Keep your back straight as well, and don't slouch, but don't make your back too stiff either. Again, there is really no set of rigid rules when it comes to mindfulness, and it can work even if you sit in a chair, as long as you are comfortable. The thing is that, if you're a beginner, getting comfortable and setting things up in this way can make for a better and more successful introduction to mindfulness.

You might also prefer to lower your chin a bit and turn your look downward, and you can also close your eyes if you wish. Closing your eyes can be useful if you're a beginner who has difficulty remaining concentrated because shutting your eyes will cut you off from anything that could get your mind wandering. Other than that, closing your eyes is not necessary. The clothes you wear are much more important when it comes to comfort. You shouldn't meditate in your jeans or other restricting clothes that keep reminding you that they are on you. Go with some loose and soft clothing.

The difference between mindfulness and many other kinds of meditation is that your objective is not to become calm or even shut off your mind. Again, the ultimate goal is just awareness in the full meaning of the word. Once you've positioned yourself the way you prefer and made yourself comfortable, you can start with the real, mental work of mindfulness.

The simplest object of focus that most beginners use is breathing. Don't try to control your breathing or breathe in a way that you think is correct. Just continue breathing as you would otherwise and observe - don't influence or analyze anything. Try to follow your breath by focusing on the physical sensations that each breath creates because this makes it easier to concentrate. Focus on things like the passage of air through your nostrils and the movements of your diaphragm and chest.

The idea is to try then and keep your attention solely on your breathing for as long as you can. With most people, especially beginners, their attention will inevitably start to shift to other things, usually their own thoughts. When this happens, you haven't failed as there is nothing to really fail at. Simply focus your attention back on the breathing, but do it gradually after a minute or so.

You must delay your re-focus because, as we mentioned above, it's important to distance yourself from your reactions. The same goes for when you start to feel an itch, or your leg gets uncomfortable. Don't react to these things right away. If your mind is particularly restless and keeps wandering, that's alright too. Rid yourself of all judgment and expectation. Your only goal is to try and be present while observing what your mind does with that.

Let the thoughts run their course without analyzing them and then try to refocus on your breath after a little while gently. Not passing any judgment toward your thoughts or the way your body reacts and not having expectations from your meditation is more difficult than it sounds. After a while, though, you will start to find it easier to stay focused for longer, and you will eventually start to feel more firmly grounded in the present moment instead of being subjugated to your mind and its scenarios and obsessions about the future or past. That's all there is to it when it comes to what mindfulness is.

Mindfulness on the Go and Additional Tips

We also mentioned that you don't really have to set aside a specific time and make mindfulness meditation a designated activity. Indeed, the alternative is to meditate on the go essentially. As we discussed, mindfulness can go hand in hand with many of the menial and seemingly mundane things you do daily. You can start to practice mindful eating, talking, exercising, walking, or even teeth brushing. There is almost no limit.

In that regard, you will use these things as the object of focus, just as you would use your breathing in the exercise we mentioned earlier. Ask yourself how often you are thinking about eating while you eat? That probably happens very rarely because you are so accustomed to it, and you tend to do it mechanically. On top of that, you have worries on your mind, and, often, your mind will wander toward those thoughts while you're having lunch.

Instead of wallowing in your thoughts, consider what you learned above and apply the same principles to your meal. Try to be aware of things like the taste, the number of chews you make, or the smell. A simple meal gives you much more opportunity to be mindful than a breathing exercise. Overall, just try to be more mindful of everything you do in daily life and always focus on the thing you are doing at that very moment. Even if you do just that, you will be practicing mindfulness. And that's the choice you have: You can formalize your meditation exercise and create a regimen for yourself, or you can introduce mindfulness into your regular life.

When it comes to your meditation if you continue to have great difficulties stopping your mind from racing when you sit down to meditate, and if these difficulties persist for a long time, there are ways to make things easier on yourself. One thing you can try is to make your meditation sessions shorter. We mentioned that you could engage in 40-minute sessions, but a mere 10-minute exercise can work just fine. When your sessions are long, and you consistently fail to focus, it might become difficult not to feel like you failed, so it's better to meditate in short bursts.

Another tool that everyone familiar with meditation will know is a mantra. Like meditation itself, mantras ("sacred sounds" or "sacred utterances") originate from India, and they are an integral part of many meditation exercises. One example is the Om mantra. In the simplest terms, this is a chant that meditators use to focus their mind and calm their thoughts. The nature of the "Om" sound is such that it can be chanter for a very long time and with varying intensity. If you are completely unfamiliar with mantras and can't understand how it sounds, there are many recordings of it on the Internet. A mantra is not just a sound to focus on and be mindful of; it also provides a certain vibration and sensation when chanted, which can assist meditation.

You can now probably see why mindfulness in all sorts of situations can be so powerful in suppressing your social anxiety. A misplaced focus has a lot to do with the onset of anxiety in each setting, and if you practice mindfulness while interacting with people, your mind can be much calmer.

You should also remember that social anxiety can be made worse by things like chronic stress, and you should know that there are many other exercises you can take up to reduce that stress and get a better command of your mind in general. There are many meditation courses, exercise groups, and personal trainers that can help you get much deeper into the world of meditation. You might find something that's perfect for you and can help change your life in many positive ways. There are also things like yoga, of course, which are constantly rising in popularity throughout the Western world.

Chapter Eight: Panic in Public Places – Ten Methods to Help You Relax

Before we get into some more ways in which you can combat your social anxiety long-term, we should also look at a few methods you can use to try and control your reactions on the spot. Although the idea behind most of these methods is just to soothe the symptoms, repeated use of some of them might also have a positive effect in the long term. Either way, whenever you succeed at overcoming an anxiety outbreak - even if it's just for a short while - you will feel strong and less helpless. Indeed, tackling your anxiety on the fly is a great way to take charge and lay the foundation for some more thorough psychological work and maintenance that you'll do later.

Of course, knowing how to subdue the symptoms at least when they arise can also make you more confident about getting into future social situations and breaking a cycle of avoidance. As already mentioned, exposure and gradual conditioning are some of the most important aspects of the struggle against SAD, so this added confidence can be a decisive boost.

Rationality Is Your Friend

As we discussed, anxiety is all about irrational fears, and rational thinking is indeed the antidote. Still, once anxiety takes over, it can be difficult to think rationally and get a grip on your racing thoughts, but you should always try to do it when your anxiety gets the better of you. Depending on how severe your anxiety is, you might not see any tangible results the first few times you try it, but after a while, you'll probably get the hang of it.

Your first step is to do your best to try and realize what's really happening. Consider your anxious reaction and try to focus on the fact that there is nothing to really fear and that you are not threatened. Your mind is fooled into perceiving a threat that isn't there, and it's triggering your flight-or-fight response for no good reason.

Furthermore, facts are your friend when you're trying to be rational. When you feel the onslaught of anxiety coming, try to focus only on the facts of the situation, *particularly positive facts*. If you're giving a presentation, for instance, and you're feeling anxious, try to think about how well-prepared you are and how knowledgeable you are on the subject. The chances are good that you're doing a great job, and the people you're presenting to are interested in the presentation, not your anxiety.

Breathe

As you know, breathing is highly relevant to anxiety. Therefore, breathing exercises are often used for all kinds of things like panic attacks, anger management, and outbreaks of anxiety. One of the simplest breathing exercises entails little more than slowing down your breathing and focusing on it.

Make sure that you are employing your diaphragm and not drawing shallow breaths. It's important to keep your breathing consistent and smooth. You should try to inhale for three to four seconds, hold the air in for three to four seconds, and then slowly exhale for the same amount of time. The point of the exercise is not to follow some golden rule about exhaling or inhaling for the exact, perfect amount of time. The idea is to keep your breathing deep and even so that your brain gets plenty of oxygen and to take your mind off the anxiety by focusing on your breathing instead.

It's important to control your breathing because it's often the first thing that suffers during an anxiety attack. Your breathing can become highly irregular, you may start to hyperventilate, or you might stop breathing altogether for a while. While breathing issues are a symptom on their own, disrupting the flow of oxygen to your brain can lead to all sorts of other symptoms of anxiety as well, such as tremors, dizziness, or even fainting. You should try to practice controlled and deep breathing at times when you're not anxious and then try to remember it when anxiety occurs again.

Interrupt Your Thoughts

When your mind starts racing, and your thoughts begin to get scary, the best thing to do is to break that negative train of thought as quickly as possible. One way to do this is with the so-called "3-3-3" rule. First, you should observe your surroundings and name the first three things you see; you can do this in your mind, if you want. Next up, scan around for three sounds and identify and name them as well. The last step is to move three parts of your body, for example: your ankle, fingers, and arm.

The idea is to distract your mind and give it something to do immediately. In fact, naming three visible things and three audible sounds might not be all that easy, depending on the environment you're in, so it can take some time and effort, which is good in terms of subduing the anxiety.

Of course, there are plenty of other things you can do to interrupt an outbreak of negative thoughts. This is highly contextual, of course, but nine times out of ten, there's something you can do to distract yourself. You can go for a little walk - even if it's just down the hallway - or you can get up and make some coffee, perhaps even clean up your desk. The important thing is to center your mind on something and get back into the moment.

Keep Busy

Indeed, keeping busy is one of the most important tips for dealing with anxiety on the fly. Don't sit around waiting for your mind to start noticing the people around you and getting ideas about what they may or may not be thinking about you. Get a jump on your own mind and focus on your work or whatever you're doing at that time.

It's a good idea to always keep some valuable distractions close by, including things like books or newspapers. If you're in a waiting room or on a crowded bus or train, reading is a very good way to focus your mind and forget about everyone around you. It's probably better than music, plus your ears won't be plugged. Of course, you can combine the two to shut off the world even more, if necessary.

Keeping busy is a good idea in general throughout your daily life, not just as a means of momentary distraction. Try and fill up your schedule with as many activities as possible and try to make them meaningful and fulfilling. The less time you spend sitting around and thinking negative thoughts, the weaker your anxiety will be. Heed this tip, especially when you find yourself anticipating an upcoming social situation. Instead of thinking about a million different scenarios where everything goes wrong, try to go for a walk or engage in a creative hobby instead.

Improve Your Posture

Like all people and a bunch of other creatures, you have a strong instinct to physically protect your vital organs when you're anxious and stressed out by a perceived threat. Usually, you won't even notice that you're doing it, but you will hunch over or cross your arms. This is a subconscious attempt to protect things like your heart and lungs, and it is an instinct left over from our cave-dwelling days.

Improving your posture can help calm you down and force your mind into accepting that there's nothing wrong and that nobody is about to attack you. Pay attention to the way you're standing or sitting next time you start feeling anxious. Try to stand up straight with your shoulders pulled back and your chest open and upward. Keep your feet apart, and don't cross your legs, especially if you're standing. Staring at the floor is another consequence of anxiety or worry, so you should try to correct that, as well.

Maintaining good is, of course, *not the cure* for social anxiety, but it's certainly something that can help. At the very least, you will project an image of confidence for others; when there are no symptoms to notice, you too will start to feel better and more peaceful.

Pull Yourself Back to Present

As you now know, social anxiety is often triggered by your notions of what's going to happen or might happen. It is the prospect of possible embarrassment or public humiliation that causes the problem, so you need to get your mind out of that fictional, future scenario and ground yourself in the present reality.

Imagine a scenario where you are late for a group meeting of some sort, and you must enter the room after everyone is already seated - a scary scenario for most sufferers of SAD. As you enter, you need to focus on the fact that you're just walking in and that being late isn't that big of a deal. Instead of obsessing over what others might be thinking or how you might get scrutinized, just focus on the task at hand. Your goal is to enter, sit, and participate, and that's all you must do and think about.

By focusing on what you're doing or are supposed to be doing, you will focus on something that's inseparable from the present moment. Furthermore, if you manage to convince yourself of the fact that you are not threatened, you might even be able to postpone your anxiety and your worries; promise yourself to address your problem later and analyze what you were worried about when you're at home.

Keep Company

If you are one of those people who have social anxiety but also happen to have a close friend or a few, you can try and keep them in your company when you feel that a situation might get difficult. Social anxiety tends to be much less intense or even non-existent when you surround yourself with people you are comfortable with.

Having a friend close by will give you something to focus on other than your anxiety. You can engage in small talk or similar interaction and keep your mind occupied by focusing on your companion instead of on your negative thoughts. Furthermore, your companion can divert the attention of others from you and make you feel less exposed. Sometimes, it's enough to be in another person's presence, but other times, it can help to tell them your problems and what you think might happen. You can try this approach next time you have an appointment or similar situation that you're anxious about, planning with your friend beforehand, agreeing to a few guidelines about dealing with an anxiety attack if it happens.

Talk to Someone About It

In this context, talking to someone about your anxiety means telling someone on the spot. If you have a friend with you, you can talk to them about how you are feeling now, but sometimes, there might also be an opportunity to talk to someone else. In fact, if you do it right, your anxiety might even be a topic that you can use to start up a conversation with a stranger.

We will look into the art of conversation and small talk later in the book, but for now, let's just say that, if you do it right, you can have a meaningful conversation about your anxiety while, at the same time, forgetting to feel anxious. It might sound counterintuitive when you're trying to forget about your anxiety, but talking about it can indeed be therapeutic. There's also a chance that you might end up talking to someone who has the same problem, and that sort of common ground can be the basis for friendship or other relationships. If you find yourself at a party or another similar social occasion, you can try and analyze the people around you and look for those who seem alone and isolated. The chances are that they are having the same issue as you are.

Think Positively

As we already discussed, defeating social anxiety has a lot to do with fighting your negative thoughts, and the importance of positive thinking can't really be stressed enough. Thinking positively is something you can try and do on the fly, not just some overall goal for your life that you need to work on over time.

You should try to relabel your negative thoughts and give them a positive spin. For instance, you can consider what we talked about earlier as your anxiety is natural and normal but misguided. Indeed, what's happening to you is that your natural survival instincts are misfiring and being misdirected – nothing more and nothing less.

It's also always a good idea to try and make things look funny in your mind. Take the people who you feel are giving you anxiety and try to imagine them in funny and unflattering circumstances. Even your anxiety itself can look funny if you try hard enough, since it is essentially an exaggeration, and exaggerations are usually an integral part of every good joke.

Focus on Others

The people responsible for your anxiety can be an endless source of distraction to help you take your mind off your anxiety. Keep in mind that the individuals who are completely confident and care-free - especially around strangers - are very rare. Whenever you meet someone, the chances are good that they are insecure about a few things. The chances are even better than they aren't giving much thought to judging and analyzing you and are, instead, thinking about the way *they appear to you.*

It's only natural to think about the impression you are giving when you meet someone, and this is how most people function. You should take advantage of that fact to help soothe your mind and take comfort in the realization that you aren't always scrutinized and judged every second of every interaction. Instead of looking at everything you are doing wrong (or *think* you are doing wrong), try focusing on the other person, for a change.

Chapter Nine: Social Confidence and Overcoming Shyness

While we have established that things like shyness are far from synonymous with social anxiety, you now know that they can certainly be connected. Shyness or perceived shyness can be symptoms of social anxiety, so there is common ground to consider between the two. Furthermore, social anxiety is also very likely to lead to low social confidence and damaged self-esteem, in general. As such, one approach to start curtailing your social anxiety is to try and boost your social confidence and learn how to carry yourself better in social situations.

With the necessary know-how and some effort, you might be able to fight through the anxiety and conduct yourself more confidently even when you are feeling anxious. Doing this can gradually get your mind used to the idea, and you might start to realize that your anxiety isn't that bad. Just managing to be functional despite your social anxiety is a great start. This isn't about faking confidence or just projecting an image, either. It's about actually boosting your confidence and overcoming a problem.

You should also note that the goal isn't to change your nature and force yourself into being extroverted when your personality is obviously that of an introvert. Not only would such efforts fail, but they would be a disservice to you and the way you really are. Ultimately, you want to be the best possible version of yourself instead of something other people think you should be. It's that kind of self-acceptance that's one of the most important steps toward building your confidence.

How It Works

With all that said, if you have social anxiety, the chances are good that you have a problem with confidence as well. The two go hand in hand, and low social confidence or overall self-esteem can often be the core of the problem when it comes to SAD. As we mentioned, it also works the other way, as social anxiety that's brought on by other causes will usually inflict self-esteem issues on you sooner or later.

Nonetheless, confidence is something that can depend on a whole range of factors, and the causes tend to run deep and vary from one individual to the next. Everyone's story is different, and those stories are usually the place to look for clues as to the possible root of the problem. Confidence and self-image problems are often the results of past trauma, childhood experiences, and sometimes even genes. The first and most important thing to take away from that is that low confidence is not your fault in any way.

Self-esteem is quite possibly one of the most important things in life. It's a trait that can determine many outcomes in life and make or break you in countless situations. Confidence or lack thereof is a trait that's omnipresent and will be reflected in almost everything you do in life. Conversations, posture, laughter, thoughts, and even walking can all reflect an individual's level of confidence. What's more, humans are quite attuned to the variations in the self-confidence of others are adept at detecting whether someone is confident or not, so it's very difficult to hide.

The problems associated with low confidence go well beyond just social situations. A poor self-image is often at the core of self-esteem issues, which means that those who lack confidence tend not to like themselves very much. Apart from making you bad at parties, this can make you lack any will at all to improve any aspect of your life. It leads to complacency and a severe lack of motivation to the point where an individual might give up on happiness altogether. This is a vicious circle because self-improvement is often one of the more effective ways to boost confidence, but if you already think very poorly of yourself, it might get difficult to see the point of such efforts.

Social confidence - or confidence in social situations, to be exact - is just one of the more specific aspects of overall self-esteem, so the two are intimately connected. Confidence will make you more assertive and easygoing, but you will also be more stable and possess a certain firmness of character. Confidence is a shield that can protect you from many things that can otherwise sting. When it comes to criticism, for instance, folks with low self-esteem tend to react in one of two ways.

One part of the crowd will feel attacked and easily lash out in a highly defensive posture, even when the criticism is constructive and even friendly. The other part tends to be sensitive and to internalize every bit of criticism as evidence that they aren't good enough, leading them to be easily discouraged. When you are confident in yourself, your worth, and your abilities, you will stand firmly and, most importantly, you will have the ability to look at yourself with cold objectivity that allows you to consider criticism, analyze it, and use it to your advantage.

All in all, a lack of social confidence can often be just a symptom of a wider self-esteem problem. When you suffer from low confidence, it will show in many areas of your life and hinder your performance at work, in relationships, and elsewhere, with or without social anxiety.

What's very important to understand is that confidence is not something you can fake. Confidence is something that truly comes from within, and people are going to notice it, whether it's low or high. More importantly, trying to fake it will not help solve any of your problems, so there's little benefit even if you manage to fool someone. Unfortunately, the misconception that you can pretend to be confident is something that's still pervasive, and it is often offered as advice by friends and family.

Instead of applying a band-aid to the problem, you should address the underlying issues and seek a permanent solution. There are many ways to improve your overall confidence, including confidence in social situations. You can adopt new ways of thinking and engage in cognitive training, introduce changes into your daily life, exercise your social skills, and do numerous other things toward this end. Working on your confidence is one of the most important things you can do to fight your social anxiety and improve your life in general. Your level of confidence and self-esteem can often be the deciding factor in getting a job, a promotion, or building relationships. As such, your level of confidence can be a help or stand in your way toward happiness.

Methods to Boost Confidence

Let's consider some tips and methods that can help you boost your confidence over time. These tips concern both the way you think and the way you behave, and most of them will require you to give them a try and go through some trial and error. The most difficult part about boosting your confidence probably has to do with your thinking. Anyone can force certain behaviors with enough strength, but internalizing new principles and concepts that you aren't used to can require a whole new level of commitment.

Social Competence

As we mentioned, social competence and confidence are linked to your overall self-esteem, so this is something you should use to your advantage. We will take a more detailed look at social skills later, especially when it comes to having conversations, but for now, let's just say that the more you work on improving your social competence, the more confident you will get.

Social competence mostly revolves around getting people interested while also having an ability to listen truly and to make them feel like you're hearing them. As you start to improve your social competence by focusing on these skills, your self-image will start to improve. Research has confirmed as much on numerous occasions, giving a variety of explanations.

Of course, as someone who has social anxiety, you probably have a problem with these things, which is why you'll learn about improving your social skills later. The most important thing to note beforehand is the connection between confidence and successful interaction. Among other things, it has to do with social acceptance, which is one of the most important factors for confidence and overall wellbeing in humans, whether we want to admit it or not.

Body Language

We already touched upon body language in the previous chapter, and with good reason. Nonverbal communication is a major part of how we interact, so it's important to practice it just as much as speech and your thoughts. Proper body language that communicates confidence and comfort will make you appear confident, but, more importantly, studies have shown that you will eventually start to feel that way as well. This is particularly true for what some people call "power poses," which generally include open poses.

There are many other subtle and not-so-subtle aspects of body language you should note. For instance, it's always important to maintain eye contact and keep your handshakes firm, yet not too forceful. Of course, eye contact and staring are not the same. Try to keep eye contact at around 60% of the time when having a conversation; this helps you express interest and make people more comfortable, apart from just making you look confident.

As far as posture goes, aside from taking wide and open poses, make sure that you stay still and composed. Don't pace around, fidget, sway, or do other similar things that communicate nervousness. The three things (maintaining eye contact, open poses, firm handshakes) are essentially the three core aspects of confident body language.

Be Kind to Yourself

As you probably know, one of the key aspects of low self-esteem and social anxiety alike is that inner voice that may be constantly berating you. It's the voice that keeps tormenting you about the things you can't change, telling you how you're not good enough, or constantly comparing you to others.

If you're going to be more confident in yourself during social or any other situations, you need, first, to start treating yourself with more kindness. This doesn't mean not fixing the fixable, of course, but it does mean cutting yourself some slack. You should think about the way you would treat a close friend or a loved one. The chances are good that you would be supportive of them and try to console and encourage them when they do something wrong. Try to apply the same approach to yourself instead of always bringing yourself down.

A good way to do this is to start focusing more on your strengths, which you certainly possess. If you don't know what your strengths are, you should find out. When you fail at something, you should be able to remember that you're good at something else and that nobody can excel at everything.

Self-Improvement

Being kind to yourself while also always trying to improve in all important ways is the best combination. Self-improvement is a broad, all-encompassing term that can include all sorts of things like changes that you can introduce into your life. You can improve yourself by improving your health, your skills, your thoughts, your fitness, or anything else you can think of.

The important thing is the effect that self-improvement has on your confidence. Low self-esteem can sometimes stem from a real shortcoming or flaw that bothers us in ourselves, and most of the time, that is fixable. Every bit of progress you make toward improving an aspect of yourself will boost your confidence, even if you don't feel it at first.

To start with, you can focus on some very basic things like your diet or eliminating some of your bad habits. Most importantly: get to work becoming the best version of yourself that you can be. In fact, it's probably best that you start small since success in these seemingly unimportant things can give you the motivation to introduce bigger changes.

Self-Care

Self-improvement often technically involves a form of self-care as well. Fixing your diet, going to the gym, and getting healthier are certainly forms of self-care that are *in addition to* self-improvement. However, self-care isn't always about putting in some sort of work toward improving yourself.

Often, self-care simply means rewarding yourself and just learning to treat yourself better. As we mentioned, harsh self-criticism or even self-loathing often go together with low self-esteem. Therefore, it's important to replace some of that harshness with positivity and enjoyment, and this best in the form of rewards, which is why it goes along well with self-improvement.

Every time you go to the gym for a workout session, or you go through a day without indulging in a bad habit or meet whatever goal you've set, you should set aside some time for yourself in the evening. Think of any activity or reward you'd particularly enjoy and let yourself have it whenever you objectively earn it. It's incredibly easy to forget to give some time to ourselves, especially with the hectic schedules that many of us must endure every day. As soon as you start treating yourself better, though, your mind will have an easier time accepting that you're not that bad after all.

Practice

These were only some of the things you can do to improve your overall confidence and social confidence. When it comes to social confidence, the most important thing is to just get as much practice as possible. You need to get this practice despite any failures that you might experience. Even if the interactions don't go well, your brain will naturally get more and more used to people, the more you interact with them.

Just being out and about can be a form of practice of your social confidence, if you don't fall into some sort of avoidant routine. When they spend enough time with social anxiety, some folks will get so good at avoidance that they might spend a whole day outside running errands with next to no real interaction with anyone. Don't avoid the social situations that might be uncomfortable – seek them out. There is a good reason it used to be called social phobia. A lot of your struggle against SAD will require you to face your fears head-on and just start exposing yourself in order to harden.

Chapter Ten: Social Anxiety and Your Relationships

Thus far, we have mostly discussed social anxiety in circumstances that are highly socially dynamic and involve multiple people, particularly strangers and large social events or daily settings that involve strangers. In this chapter, we will look at how social anxiety relates to your relationships and how it can affect them. In fact, we will consider t the impact of social anxiety on human relationships, in general, and some tips on how to deal with it in these contexts.

It's certainly clear to you by now that social anxiety tends to occur mostly when strangers are involved. We mentioned earlier that socially anxious folks could often have a close friend or two whom they are comfortable with, and it's possible that you are in a similar situation. Still, social anxiety is something that can affect relationships, both potential and already existing ones. The greatest and most common difficulty is in forming new relationships, but there are ways in which your existing relationships – even those that you have cherished for years – can suffer.

Social Anxiety and Relationships

Of course, if social anxiety poses a problem for human relationships would be very intuitive, but there's a bit more to it than that. In the lives of most people, there exist relationships that predate the development of social anxiety. This primarily includes parents, siblings, and other family members, but it can also include childhood friends. These are the relationships we just mentioned when we talked about how socially anxious people can still be close to someone.

One way in which social anxiety can damage a pre-existing, functional relationship is by gradually driving a wedge between the two people. Imagine, for instance, a relationship such as a friendship or any other kind where the other person is highly sociable and outgoing while you are socially anxious and withdrawn. Apart from when you hang out one-on-one, you would mostly be inclined not to go out and socialize, turning down many invitations and gradually seeing less and less of that person. As close as they can be to us, our friends and loved ones can often be blind to our problems, especially subtle ones like anxiety. This is just one of the ways in which certain relationships can turn cold because of your anxiety.

Another problem that you might be well-aware of is that socially anxious people often find it difficult to discuss and express their feelings, *let alone articulate them.* This inability to communicate one's true feelings, including needs and desires, is what ends many - if not most – relationships, and the problem is especially pronounced with anxiety. It's not just that the anxiety has a direct effect on your ability to communicate. The issue is also in how your social anxiety has deprived you of meaningful contact and deeper interaction with others for so long. The inability to communicate and express emotions can simply be the result of a lack of experience.

According to some experts, this inability to express feelings and communicate on a deeper level is SAD's most damaging aspect when it comes to relationships. This was researched and supported by a 2018 Canadian study conducted at the University of British Columbia by Lynn Alden and other experts. The goal of this study was to challenge the traditional view that social anxiety should be treated by focusing solely on the reduction of avoidant behavior. The study postulated that the relationship deficit in social anxiety and the inability to express or articulate true feelings was just as important.

Yet another Canadian study - conducted at Western University by Christian Hahn - investigated the connection between social anxiety and relationship satisfaction too. As you would expect, the study found that relationship satisfaction was lower when social anxiety was involved. It was found that social anxiety was particularly detrimental for the trust and support in romantic relationships.

One of the main reasons for this is the sensitivity that social anxiety causes. This is the sensitivity toward criticism and fragile self-esteem, as we discussed earlier in the book. These things can get bad enough that even your romantic partner can start to appear like they are hostile, overly judgmental, and trying to humiliate you. Your partner might be trying to give you advice or help you in some way because they care, but to an anxious mind, help can often look like an attack. On top of that, the strong negativity bias and outright self-loathing that some socially anxious folks suffer from can make them deaf to positive feedback.

Beyond close friendships and romantic relationships, there are also relationships that you have with folks like your relatives. Relatives, particularly those from your extended family, exist in a sort of a grey area when it comes to closeness. On paper, they are to be considered close because they are part of the family, but in practice, most people see their relatives only periodically. This drives a wedge between you and them and can make family gatherings very stressful when you have social anxiety.

Furthermore, family gatherings can be such a circus of judgment and scrutiny that you might feel like you're being interrogated. Indeed, relatives always want updates, and they will pass their opinions on all sorts of things that concern you and your life. They will often compare you to others, ask you intimate questions, and really get under your skin - *even when they mean well.* Many people don't particularly enjoy that, let alone socially anxious folks! On top of that, it isn't uncommon for relatives to bring their friends or significant others to such gatherings, which means you can be forced to interact with strangers as well as members of your extended family.

With all that said, the most common way in which social anxiety affects relationships is still the way it diminishes your odds of establishing future ones. People who don't have social anxiety can go through break-ups, lose friends, get estranged from family, et cetera, but they will always be able to strike up a conversation and meet new people to fill the void. If you have both social anxiety and a close friend or a romantic partner in your life, then you know all too well how important and difficult to replace they are.

That's not to say that true friend is easy to come by or replace for anyone, but there is a whole other degree of hopelessness when your social anxiety keeps you down after a break-up or a loss of friendship.

Dealing with It

Obviously, the best way to deal with the damage that your social anxiety inflicts on your relationships is to deal with the social anxiety itself. What we have discussed and will continue to discuss after this chapter will help you in that regard, but you can still take steps to overcome anxiety-related issues in your relationships.

As you have probably gathered from what we talked about a little earlier, communication is paramount in romantic relationships. It's crucial in all human relations, of course, but romantic relationships are especially intimate, and, as such, they rest on the couple's ability to communicate on a deeper level than they would with anyone else in their lives. When two people function together, they communicate on all levels, verbal and nonverbal alike. They can weather through difficulties and misunderstandings because they know and understand each other, especially when it comes to all those quirks and weaknesses that people carry.

One of the most important things in this regard is to build and nurture trust. The only way you can strengthen that trust is by giving it a try. If you are intimate with someone and you care deeply about them, then you must trust them to make it work. You can start with some very simple things, such as honesty and the highest level of openness you can muster. Whenever you see a certain problem or anything bothers you, you must get on top of it as soon as you can and talk to your partner about it.

Don't let such issues lie dormant and fester under the surface. When things are bottled up, pressure builds, and those things that are left unsaid will often come back later and cause even more problems. They might also return as contempt, spite, and all manner of nastiness. All in all, every problem should be discussed and cleared up as soon as it arises. Not only will this solve more problems, but each time you do it, trust improves.

Communication that includes criticism should kept up to a certain standard. If you are sensitive to criticism and tend to be set off by such things, you should avoid being too critical of your partner, as well. Simply treat your partner with the same level of respect that you expect for yourself. Problems need to be talked about, *not yelled about.* Certainly, this is sometimes easier said than done, but with a bit of mindfulness and positive thought realignment, you should be able to control yourself - even when your partner can't.

That's really all there is to building trust: communicating in an effective and meaningful way while applying the golden rule. Once you feel that you trust your partner, but the problems associated with your anxiety keep coming back, you can try dealing with other issues.

You need to sit down and have an honest discussion with yourself concerning all the ways in which you could improve. To that end, consider all the things we have discussed, improving the way you think and all the other tips that have to do with behavior. Depending on your case, some of these things might help you, while others might not be as relevant. If you are unsure where to start, you can also talk to your partner about it, *if there is trust.*

Romantic relationships are a good place to be in when trying to beat your social anxiety. If you have both, you should also consider how lucky you are. For millions of people all over the world, being unable to find and establish such a relationship is the most excruciating aspect of their social anxiety. As such, you should consider your relationship as something that is already giving you a head-start.

When it comes to things like those pesky family gatherings we mentioned, the best way to deal with those situations is with the tips discussed before and after this chapter. Your best bet is to focus on that one relative or family member whom you are the most comfortable with. If you can relate to at least one person, that's an excellent, seamless inroad into a group, or at the very least, a conversation with such a person can help distract you.

With social anxiety and its relationship problems, friendships, and romantic relationships have a fair amount of common ground. Just like intimate relationships, true friendship entails trust, support, and communication. As such, a lot of what we have just discussed applies to friendships as well.

When it comes to romantic relationships or marriage, consider professional help. There is a specific type of cognitive-behavioral therapy, called CBT-R, wherein "R" stands for "relationships." This form of therapy for social anxiety with an emphasis on relationships has been found to work in studies such as the University of British Columbia study.

The availability of this approach might vary depending on where you live, but if all else fails, then it might be worth it to travel a bit to seek such help. There is nothing wrong with looking for help from an outside party, and it's a good idea to discuss it with your significant other, garnering their support and understanding which, in turn, provides you with a significant boost towards success.

Chapter Eleven: Small Talk and Other Social Skills for Introverts

Socially anxious individuals and most introverts can always benefit from learning about social skills that they would like to have. It's not always just about freeing yourself from fear and anxiety; though though that is certainly a great achievement, it probably won't magically make you adept at socializing overnight. This is especially true if the important developmental period in your life - the time when you were supposed to master these social skills - was marred by social anxiety and withdrawn living.

In that case, it might be necessary to catch up on some of that knowledge and learn some useful social skills to get you started in reclaiming your social life. It might be difficult at first, but once you get out there and see a couple of instances of success, things will often take a natural course, and you will be well on your way toward full recovery. We will take this chapter to discuss some of those useful social skills, especially those that relate to communication, and some additional tips to help you along the way.

Small Talk

We've already briefly mentioned small talk and how introverts, extroverts, socially anxious people, and others deal with it. What we didn't mention, however, is that despite how trivial it might be on the surface, small talk plays a very important part in the way human beings interact and communicate.

First and foremost, it provides a foundation for the interaction and familiarization between people because it plays an important part in our social rituals. Many acquaintances begin with chit-chat, and whether that acquaintance becomes something more will often depend on what happens during that initial stage exchanging pleasantries. As such, more advanced layers of communication and interaction can often depend on small talk. Being a basic and relatively simple social skill, small talk is also a great entry point for folks who wish to get back at the helm of their social life and start to practice their rusty or non-existent social skills.

Pleasant chit-chat is also a tool that can help calm you down in nervous social situations. As you know, many people will resort to small talk whenever they feel nervous or awkward in a situation. This is a very natural response, and it goes to show you how important it can be in terms of leveling things out and maintaining stability in social interaction. If you master it, small talk will always be that one card you can fall back on when things start to get anxious or awkwardly quiet.

It's also worth mentioning that small talk doesn't necessarily entail true conversations. Often, chit-chat will entail only a relatively quick exchange of remarks that will be just enough to get things moving along and make a situation more comfortable for the parties involved. In fact, you will mostly want to keep it that way as well. Don't go into too much detail or force conversations, especially conversations about serious topics.

As someone who struggles with social interaction, these short bursts of small talk, you can have will serve as a way for you to practice and get a foot in the door, so to speak. Just like mindfulness, it's something you should introduce into your daily life. You can think of situations like supermarket queues, going to the bank or DMV, or waiting for a train. All these situations will give often give you an opportunity to practice small talk. The best part is that they involve complete strangers whom you will never see again, so even if an embarrassing situation occurs, there will be no real consequence, and you can forget about it five minutes later!

In order to get enough practice, you will have to switch from waiting for small talk to *initiating it*. If you are unsure how you can initiate small talk in daily life, you should consider things like asking for directions or getting into situations with very active, large social gatherings - as scary as that might sound.

Consider a setting like a club or a rally of some sort. These situations involve a lot of strangers and a very high probability of interaction, but the important thing to note is your position therein. Namely, you will be nothing but a stranger in a sea of strangers, which can be a good thing. As counterintuitive as it sounds, crowds can be much less scary when you have SAD than one-on-one or being a stranger in a group of three to four people. There is simply so much attention going around in all directions that you will be protected by the statistics alone. It also means you can get to practice small talk with people who will forget all about it in five minutes if you cut off the interaction.

Overall, always keep in mind that small talk can easily spark a meaningful conversation and, eventually, friendship or even a romantic relationship. It might sound like a cliché, but it happens: people just click sometimes. If you stay positive and aren't forceful, you can rest assured that nothing bad came come from your efforts to engage in chit-chat with others. If someone reacts in a hostile or overly unpleasant manner, it won't be your fault.

When you strike up a conversation with someone agreeable, and you feel pleasant, small talk can go on for a longer time. In no time at all, you can find yourself moving from talking about the weather to really getting to know a person.

Advanced Communication

Being good at communicating with people is so much more than mastering small talk, of course. Knowing how to focus, listen, express, and present yourself with friendliness and style are all important skills to take communication beyond just small talk.

When it comes to communication with others, start with becoming a good listener. As someone who struggles with social interaction, you can gain a lot from just listening to people, regardless of who initiated the conversation. For one, when you let the other person do the talking, you are shifting the focus of the conversation and most of the thinking to them. This will give you some room to breathe, but it will also help you learn a thing or two about body language.

To be a good listener also means knowing how and when to react and nudge the conversation forward or even in the desired direction. You will need restraint, maybe more than you can anticipate. If your social anxiety has deprived you of interaction and meaningful conversations with people for a long time, you might be very eager to get talking, especially when you sense that the other person is beginning to take a genuine interest in you; it can be very tempting to talk on and on. To be a listener, you need to resist this urge and avoid inserting yourself into everything that the other person says.

Asking questions is an important part of keeping a conversation going. This is another reason why it's good to let the other person talk. The more they say, the more inspiration and material you will have for simple questions related to what they are talking about. You can insert these questions here and there to keep a conversation going along smoothly. Listening and gathering information will also help you make your questions engaging and original instead of mundane, making it look like you're only asking to seem nice or feign interest.

When a conversation starts running out of steam, and you need to give it a little push, you should ask questions that can't be answered with just a yes or a no. You should try and make those questions revolve around who, what, where, when, and why. Questions that start that way tend to give much more room for conversation and continuation of the discussion.

Most people love a good listener, so it's a good start if you want people to think you're a nice, pleasant person. Another disarming tactic is a simple compliment or two, being sure not to overdo it; make sure you only give sincere comments, and only when you really feel they are truly adequate. It's a very good way to set you up as friendly early in the conversation.

Eventually, you will also get into a situation where you will be the one who's supposed to lead a conversation. Expressiveness becomes very important if you are to get the message across while also keeping people interested and the conversation flowing. Try to be as descriptive- yet as simple and to-the-point - as possible when telling a story or describing anything.

In order to be more expressive and have your conversations go smoother, you might also want to try and create a script of sorts for how you want a conversation to develop. Of course, you can't script out the actual conversation with all its sentences, but you can write down a list or something similar, outlining your goals for when you have a conversation with someone. These goals can include certain topics you want to discuss, questions you want to ask, and other things. It's a good idea to know exactly what you want to accomplish by talking to someone.

Lastly, when it comes to expressing yourself, it's not all about the way you talk, either. Showing style in the way you clothe yourself, for instance, can leave a positive impression and impact the conversations you're having in a good way. In turn, this can also have a positive effect on your overall confidence, so the style can be very important indeed.

Overall, the most important thing is just to start conversing with people. Depending on your SAD and past record, it might be very difficult at first, but the illusion that conversations and strangers are scary is best dispelled by facing that fear head-on. As soon as you've had a few conversations, you will start to feel more at ease, especially if you started those conversations.

Other Tips

In general, if you aren't overly trusting, the best way to approach people is to consider everyone a potential friend whom you just didn't find yet. Keep in mind that there are many other people you could run into who also suffer from social anxiety. Your similar experiences can be a conversation topic and a starting point for a great friendship, but it can also make it exceptionally difficult to get things going. Therefore, it's important to be friendly, pleasant, and smile whenever you can. That's not to say that you should fake a smile to impress someone, quite the contrary – an earnest smile can make anyone feel more at ease when they interact with you.

One important thing you can do in the way of improving your social skills is to observe and learn. You will inevitably come across people who are confident and very adept at socializing, and you will be able to learn a lot just by observing them. When it comes to social skill and confidence, there are some things that can hardly be described with words, so you will have to learn them on the fly. When you see someone who socializes with ease, take note of their body language and the way they speak. You will see many of the tips you've learned in this book come seamlessly into a real-life scenario.

It's important to understand that your goal isn't to fundamentally change who you are. If you are introverted, it's only natural not to be the life of the party and a master of social skills. Your goal is to rid yourself of all fear and to be able to function when social situations do arise, not to become suddenly ultra-sociable. It's perfectly fine to skirt being the center of attention, staying reserved, and not going out every night. If this is who you are, so be it, and you should wear your nature with pride.

Once you defeat your social anxiety and become more confident, your introversion can become something that's appealing. This is true both for men and women. Introversion can give certain people an interesting aura of mystery and enigma that attracts people. The old cliché about being yourself still holds true and will continue to be so. When you start to like yourself, and when your fear of judgment has subsided, you will find that other people will have an easier time liking you, too.

Another important tip when you're trying to improve your social skills is to do your best to make your strengths and virtues come to light. Take a moment to consider what these strengths of yours are. Maybe you are good at listening to people and giving them advice, or perhaps you are very knowledgeable about certain interesting topics. Whatever it is, try to make it come to the spotlight instead of trying to pretend that you're an extrovert to fit in. That would be the road toward being a show-off - and nobody likes that.

Remember that, as an introvert, you still need that downtime you spend alone to recharge. When you are trying to hone your social skills, you should always approach situations with a fresh and eager mind. If you force yourself into too much social interaction in a short span of time, you might get to feeling burned out, and that will make interaction much more difficult and disheartening.

As you can see, there really isn't all that much to it. You must practice and keep on practicing; your social skills will eventually have to come back to you. Even if you throw yourself back into society abruptly, shock your mind and body, and encounter a few abysmal failures, it will still count as practice. Social skills are like riding a bicycle in that you have it in you, but you just need to commit to it and not get discouraged - even if you fall flat on your face. The more you talk to people, the easier it will get, and - most importantly - you will get to see how little there is to fear.

You will also see just how many other people have a whole range of problems that they struggle with, and that can do more to make you feel less isolated than the interactions themselves. You will quickly realize that strangers aren't these perfect beings who have it all figured out, who all belong to some club that you need to join while they judge your every move. A million people will have a million different struggles; getting to learn about them will be one of the more fascinating aspects of your journey.

Chapter Twelve: Breaking Out of Your Comfort Zone

As you have probably gathered in the course of this book, beating your social anxiety will require you to traverse beyond your comfort zone many times and in many ways. This can entail copious amounts of fear, stress, frustration, and failure, but all of it will be necessary if you are to rewire your brain and rid yourself of your fears permanently.

Given enough time, your social anxiety can completely convince you that you are comfortable in isolation and that you really don't have to change anything. This illusion is one of the more dangerous aspects of social anxiety, and it can exist for a long time. At some point, though, the illusion is broken when you realize how much you have missed out on and how many areas of your life have come to be affected by it. Since you are reading this book, the chances are good that this has happened to you.

What Is Your Comfort Zone?

Perhaps the fact that this is an illusion is what makes the term "comfort zone" a bit inaccurate too. Namely, a state that you were conditioned to be in because of your fears might not qualify as a very comfortable one, once you take a closer look at least. There is comfort, and then, *there is complacency.*

Indeed, the difference between the two is significant yet often overlooked. Most people don't make that distinction, and it can lead to them being misunderstood, particularly when they give advice to introverts. As we discussed, introverts such as yourself are naturally more comfortable in calm environments and among few friends, and there is nothing wrong with that. As such, when you are advised to get out of your comfort zone, what's meant is not that you need to stop being you. Instead, the idea is to get out of what some people call the "complacency zone."

The complacency zone is the illusion we mentioned earlier. It is a place where our fear and anxiety force us to go and hide in order to avoid having to deal with the discomfort of those situations that we dread. When you find that you have established a daily routine around that fear and constructed your days in a way that allows you to avoid social situations, you have settled in the complacency zone. Has your social anxiety made you order food instead of going out to get it yourself? Do you find that you often come up with weak excuses not to go out when a friend calls you?

It's that avoidance that keeps your social anxiety going strong and getting stronger over time. And because you think you are avoiding fear and stress, you begin to think that you are comfortable in this avoidance. In reality, though, you are becoming complacent and are accomplishing nothing but allowing what is essentially a curable disease to take hold of you and control your life.

In fact, you're not even avoiding your fear, as much it as might feel that way. Your fear always continues to be present, and it continues to rule your life even though you've minimized the amount of anxiety you feel. As such, your complacency zone is a place where you accomplish nothing and are, in fact, probably making things worse. This is a status quo that you don't want to uphold if you wish for things to get better in a meaningful way. You and your social anxiety aren't a unique case of this either. Plenty of people are stuck in some sort of complacency zone that's relevant to their problems.

The way you think and behave can be indicative of whether you are stuck in this zone. For instance, do you often find that you tend to put off solving certain problems, preferring instead to pretend like the problems aren't there? A complacency zone also comes with a whole lot of rationalization where you might be looking for excuses and seemingly rational explanations for your avoidance and inactivity. Your complacency and fear might make you turn down an offer to meet up with a friend, but you might not tell yourself that. Namely, when we are stuck in this situation, it's easy to come up with a million seemingly rational explanations, such as that we were tired or too busy when we know deep down that this isn't true.

As you can see, there isn't a whole lot of "comfort" that goes into any of this, just self-delusion and stagnation. Another reason why it's important to understand the difference between this and a "comfort zone" is that you want to rely on your strengths in the struggle against social anxiety. For instance, when an introvert gets to thinking that he or she is supposed to act like an extrovert in order to leave their perceived comfort zone, that person will set themselves up for failure.

You have enough on your plate with your social anxiety, so it's not always a good idea to put yourself in situations that don't agree with your personality on top of that. As an introvert, it might be better for you to try and practice your social skills in situations where your innate introvert strengths can shine. Think of things like your concentration, introspection, and other things you're good at.

If we use these definitions and consider the difference between comfort and complacency, it becomes clear that your actual comfort zone is not necessarily a bad thing. Keeping all this in mind, consider the nature of extroverts for a moment. Being surrounded by lots of people and getting a lot of interaction is what we would consider an extrovert's comfort zone. Of course, people don't tend to encourage extroverts to get out of this particular "comfort zone," and extroverts are encouraged instead. As such, misguided advice ends up encouraging introverts to quite literally leave their natural "comfort zone" and then pretend to be comfortable in that of extroverts.

With all that said, it's true that most people simply use the term "comfort zone" as a synonym for what we just described as the complacency zone. Now that we've cleared up the important difference and real meaning of both, we will do the same from here onward to keep things simple.

Much of what we've discussed in this book already entails breaking out of your comfort zone. Starting conversations, taking up meditation, addressing the troublesome thoughts you carry in your mind, and a few other things we mentioned can all be uncomfortable when you have SAD. As with many other things in life, the most difficult part for many people is just to get started.

Avoidance can get so familiar, and your mind can get so used to it that you completely forget what it's like to be in any other state. It might seem unbelievable to those of you with only mild social anxiety, but some folks have indulged their fear and been avoidant for so long that even the most basic of interactions can appear impossible. That's why you might start thinking that you are more comfortable staying inside and cutting the world off.

By breaking out of that idea of comfort and facing your fears, you will find that your mind might just as easily get accustomed to interaction as it did to isolation. Even when struggling with personality disorders, humans still have an incredible capacity to adapt and get used to new situations, especially when they are routine. If you find the strength to make those initial steps, you will find that *anything is possible.*

Breaking Out

So, how do you get out of your comfort zone? It will generally entail assertiveness and decisive action or, in a word, boldness. Still, you can be methodical, systematic, and gradual with how you depart from your comfort zone. There are numerous strategies, tips, and changes you can try out, particularly when it comes to social anxiety.

Preparing for the First Step

This doesn't mean preparing to make a movie in each moment when you're already in a certain situation. It means preparing your mind and body during your days when the moment to act comes. You can prepare yourself to leave your comfort zone in many ways, some of which we've already discussed. Self-improvement is certainly one example. It can help many folks if they are fit, for instance, so picking up a workout regimen and getting yourself in shape can always make it easier to break out of your socially anxious comfort zone.

It's also important to get some things straight with yourself. For one, consider what that most problematic part about yourself, which you want to change, is. Try to pinpoint the exact behavior that you want to stop in the future. This can be something very simple and small just to get you started. Think about a certain thing that you do to indulge your social anxiety, such as avoiding talking on the phone. Pick any individual piece of your avoidant behavior and focus on breaking the cycle the next time an opportunity arises. The moment you act and say no to your avoidance, even in the simplest way, will be the moment you begin your new life.

Create a Plan of Action

Something else that's useful is to have reasons for doing what you do. That way, if the going gets tough or you get cold feet, you always have those reasons to fall back on. Always keep your reasons and your overall goals in mind, using them as a source of energy.

Furthermore, it's good always to have a relatively detailed and solid plan for the things that you want to do. Are you intending to break out of your comfort zone by applying for a new job and going to the interview? In that case, make a plan that includes all the things you want to say how you are going to present yourself, and all the other parts that go into it. You should plan for when things go south, such as if the interviewers ask you a trick question or expose your weaknesses.

Without obsessing over how you are going to get anxious, you should make a clear plan and a backup plan so that you're never caught in the headlights. Unexpected turns can leave you stumped and trapped in an anxious cycle. The objective of being prepared is not just to succeed but also to deal with failure and pick yourself up for that next attempt. Wherever you go, venture out with a plan.

Adjust Your Expectations

First and foremost, you should, of course, expect lots of discomfort and brace yourself for numerous failures, just in case. We did mention that taking the first step is most important, but that doesn't mean you should expect things to just magically come together as soon as you take a step in the right direction.

Try to consider all the possible ways in which a situation can go, writing those scenarios down. This can often have a calming effect because it makes things seem less scary than they were in your head. Furthermore, we are not talking about obsessively worrying about a scenario; simply try to be as objective as possible, thinking of a few ways that your venture outside the comfort zone can go. The purpose of that is to show you that even the worst scenario is probably harmless and won't have any lasting ramifications, giving you more motivation to do it.

The most important thing is not to have expectations that are too high. In fact, that's more important even than having them be too low. Don't set yourself up for disappointment because that can be more discouraging than any bad scenario you can think of. Consider both the good and possible bad outcomes and try to change your perspective from worrying to curiosity. Try to make yourself simply curious to see what happens when you step out of that zone.

Don't Think Too Much

Opportunities to break out of your comfort zone can often appear out of nowhere. You might find yourself outside, just going about your day, when suddenly, there is an opportunity to interact with someone and establish meaningful contact. Of course, these chances are especially common when you go out for the night, for instance.

If you decide that approaching someone and starting a conversation is your preferred way of breaking out of your comfort zone, you should apply something that some folks refer to as the "three-second rule." This rule applies to all sorts of ways to break out of comfort zones, not just in social situations. It simply prescribes to wait no more than three seconds before acting.

The goal is not to let your mind fall into its old pattern of overanalyzing and panicking over a million ways in which you can embarrass yourself. If you see someone you want to talk to, simply tell yourself that this is the opportunity you've been waiting for, not something to fear, and then make a move. Certainly, this is easier said than done, and it might take some practice before you succeed, but the results can be incredible. When you don't give your fearful mind enough time to shut you down, you might quickly find yourself in a pleasant conversation, realizing how little there was to fear. This is one of the best ways to strike against social anxiety.

Stop Being an Observer in Your Life

Ask yourself one simple question: Do you want to take charge and play an active role in your life, or would you rather be a bystander to your own story? There are only a few things that can lead you down a road of passivity the way social anxiety can. This disorder wants you to shut yourself off and let your life pass you by.

It wants you to sit at home, adopt a passive existence where you just wait for things to happen instead of making them happen.

As comfortable as that might appear to your conditioned mind, it won't work out in the end. To get anywhere in life, you first need to start moving, and it doesn't matter how small those initial steps are, *as long as you make them.* If you see people doing the things you want to do, ask yourself what's really stopping you. One of the most important things you have learned from this book is that social anxiety is something you can and must beat on your own. It's not a problem that others can solve for you. You must stop being the audience to your own life and start assuming the main, active role that was always meant for you.

Conclusion

As you can see, your social anxiety is a burden you can throw off over time. Although nobody's story is quite the same, your first source of comfort can be the realization that your problem is a very common one. What's also entirely likely is that there are many, many people out there whose social anxiety is much worse than yours. Nonetheless, even they can overcome it, and they do, often completely on their own.

If you do have support from a friend or beloved family member, though, that's even better. You should talk to them about your problem, especially if they are extroverted and don't have any such issues. Having those that are close to you understand what you're going through can be incredibly encouraging, but it can also make your life and your recovery easier.

You also shouldn't refrain from seeking professional help from a psychiatrist or therapist. You can always schedule a session at least as a means of diagnosis and to have a little conversation. It never even occurs to many people that they could seek out such help, much less that it could help them, but they are usually wrong. Therapists can be incredibly adept at getting to the root of your problems, and you might be surprised by the help they can provide in a short period of time. What's more, you might find that they are quick to catch on to things that you thought nobody would ever understand.

All in all, your time has come to a stop despairing and especially to stop letting this disorder run your life and take the joy right out of it. You now know that you don't have to live this way and that it only takes a bit of effort and some patience on your part. With an informed and positive attitude, you might turn into a whole new person!

Resources

https://www.psycom.net/social-anxiety-disorder-overview

https://adaa.org/understanding-anxiety/social-anxiety-disorder

https://www.webmd.com/anxiety-panic/guide/mental-health-social-anxiety-disorder#1

https://socialphobia.org/social-anxiety-disorder-definition-symptoms-treatment-therapy-medications-insight-prognosis

https://www.mayoclinic.org/diseases-conditions/social-anxiety-disorder/symptoms-causes/syc-20353561

https://www.youtube.com/watch?v=BcRobzrfc98

https://introvertdear.com/news/anxious-introverts-fears/

https://www.psychologytoday.com/us/blog/the-secret-lives-introverts/201805/15-signs-anxious-introvert

https://www.wisebread.com/7-social-situations-all-introverts-fear

https://www.healthline.com/health/how-to-calm-anxiety#3

https://www.verywellmind.com/managing-panic-disorder-in-public-2584185

https://www.healthline.com/health/mental-health/panic-attacks-in-public#4

https://www.webmd.com/mental-health/features/ways-to-reduce-anxiety

https://verilymag.com/2018/12/signs-of-social-anxiety-social-anxiety-disorder-anxiety-introvert

https://www.youtube.com/watch?v=n5Xsk6vwzYY

https://www.huffpost.com/entry/difference-social-anxiety-introversion_n_5adf5e6de4b07560f3961226

https://www.melbournechildpsychology.com.au/blog/distinguishing-behaviours-the-difference-between-shyness-introversion-and-social-anxiety/

https://www.quietrev.com/the-4-differences-between-introversion-and-social-anxiety/

https://www.promisesbehavioralhealth.com/addiction-recovery-blog/introvert-shy-socially-anxious-whats-the-difference/

https://introvertdear.com/what-is-an-introvert-definition/

https://www.verywellmind.com/signs-you-are-an-introvert-2795427

https://psychcentral.com/blog/treating-social-anxiety-with-meditation-and-mindfulness-training/

https://www.verywellmind.com/meditation-for-social-anxiety-3024211

https://missionbe.org/faq/?gclid=Cj0KCQiAvJXxBRCeARIsAMSkAppB8mkjiygV7Gu4HMMpnF8FK5YnBC81SJpET4pbC7TbR2JtF_U6-L0aAkgPEALw_wcB

https://www.mindful.org/meditation/mindfulness-getting-started/

https://www.alustforlife.com/soul/you-are-alive/10-mindfulness-tips-to-help-you-live-a-more-peaceful-life?gclid=Cj0KCQiApaXxBRDNARIsAGFdaB_N1hDQZTikREC_dw6tnrGUh4hDNxke05cEVuaeSm6sTM0zNVGYXrwaApweEALw_wcB

https://www.youtube.com/watch?v=ld_QpsD0qpk

https://www.mindful.org/mindfulness-how-to-do-it/

https://www.youtube.com/watch?v=xsCxltuzmDI

https://www.youtube.com/watch?v=CjsZfYjaTUQ

https://www.elitedaily.com/p/how-introverts-can-make-small-talk-less-painful-more-meaningful-according-to-experts-8917603

https://www.lifehack.org/articles/lifestyle/7-epic-strategies-for-introverts-by-introverts-to-ignite-your-social-skills.html
http://elitemanmagazine.com/10-tips-to-becoming-more-social-as-an-introvert/
https://www.youtube.com/watch?v=Jv_Qjis_ZXo
https://www.youtube.com/watch?v=xIE_w0QLyiE
https://www.youtube.com/watch?v=2yRVP9PHnEE
https://www.wikihow.com/Be-Socially-Confident
https://www.lifehack.org/372358/5-ways-start-building-social-confidence-today
https://thriveglobal.com/stories/comfort-zone-or-complacency-zone-please-stop-scaring-introverts/
https://nationalsocialanxietycenter.com/2018/02/16/overcoming-social-anxiety-choosing-step-outside-comfort-zone/
https://herpaperroute.com/get-out-of-your-comfort-zone/
https://www.psychologytoday.com/intl/blog/cutting-edge-leadership/201405/introversion-5-strategies-pushing-out-your-comfort-zone
https://www.youtube.com/watch?v=3jy-44L7_bo
https://www.youtube.com/watch?v=cmN4xOGkxGo
https://www.health.harvard.edu/blog/do-i-have-anxiety-or-worry-whats-the-difference-2018072314303
https://www.psychologytoday.com/us/blog/the-squeaky-wheel/201603/10-crucial-differences-between-worry-and-anxiety
https://www.verywellmind.com/fear-and-anxiety-differences-and-similarities-2584399
https://www.psychiatry-uk.com/anxiety-explained/
https://www.psychologytoday.com/us/blog/science-choice/201812/anxiety-vs-fear
https://www.goodtherapy.org/blog/psychpedia/trigger
https://www.verywellmind.com/which-situations-trigger-anxiety-3024887
http://overcomingsocialanxiety.com/common-social-anxiety-triggers/

https://www.youtube.com/watch?v=mmPMwYHtoD4

https://www.helpguide.org/articles/anxiety/social-anxiety-disorder.htm

https://lifehacker.com/what-anxiety-actually-does-to-you-and-what-you-can-do-a-1468128356

https://www.psychologytoday.com/us/blog/wander-woman/201507/5-steps-managing-your-emotional-triggers

https://www.inc.com/nate-klemp/try-this-neuroscience-based-technique-to-shift-your-mindset-from-negative-to-positive-in-30-seconds.html

https://www.psychologytoday.com/us/blog/women-s-mental-health-matters/201509/7-ways-deal-negative-thoughts

https://www.verywellmind.com/what-are-negative-automatic-thoughts-3024608

https://www.psychologytoday.com/us/blog/the-mindful-self-express/201708/3-negative-thinking-patterns-avoid-what-do-instead

https://www.psychologytoday.com/intl/blog/fulfillment-any-age/201806/is-social-anxiety-getting-in-the-way-your-relationships

https://psychcentral.com/blog/you-can-stop-social-anxiety-from-ruining-your-relationships/

https://www.psychologytoday.com/intl/blog/fulfillment-any-age/201501/6-ways-get-more-comfortable-others-and-yourself

https://shynesssocialanxiety.com/nervous-around-relatives/

https://www.verywellmind.com/managing-social-anxiety-disorder-at-work-3024812

https://www.anxiety.org/if-social-anxiety-disorder-affects-your-romantic-relationships